THE DOWNING LEGACY

Lee and Blanche Downing
February 1927

THE DOWNING LEGACY
Six Decades at Rift Valley Academy

✦

Mary Andersen Honer

iUniverse, Inc.
New York   Bloomington

The Downing Legacy
Six Decades at Rift Valley Academy

iUniverse books may be ordered through booksellers or by contacting:

iUniverse
1663 Liberty Drive
Bloomington, IN 47403
www.iuniverse.com
1-800-Authors (1-800-288-4677)

The views expressed in this work are solely those of the author and do not necessarily reflect the views of the publisher, and the publisher hereby disclaims any responsibility for them.

ISBN: 978-1-4502-1366-0 (pbk)
ISBN: 978-1-4502-1368-4 (cloth)
ISBN: 978-1-4502-1367-7 (ebook)

Printed in the United States of America

iUniverse rev. date: 5/27/2010

****
Cover
Cape Chestnut flower
Calodendrum capense

Herbert Downing enjoyed his camera and often tried to get a good picture of the Cape Chestnut that grew at Kijabe, according to his daughter, Ruth Ann. He never felt he quite captured the beautiful color. Hopefully this cover does.

The Cape Chestnut tree is graceful and slow growing, bearing lilac-blue flowers twice a year. It is drought-hardy and provides a useful yellow timber. It grows to fifty feet in height. Indigenous in Kikuyu and Kamba country of Kenya. Rare in West Uganda and common in northern Tanzania.

Cover photograph by Mary Honer. Photo at Kijabe, June 2009

In Memory of

Lee and Blanche Downing,

Herbert and Mildred Downing,

and

Kenneth and Ivy Downing,

who together gave over sixty years in the service

of children at the Rift Valley Academy

and

to their children:

Gayle, Glenn, Edwin, Ruth Ann, and Martin,

and

Daphne, David, Dorothy, Lee, and Victor,

who shared their parents with so many others.

Contents

Acknowledgments

Several years ago I was visiting with friends in Kenya, who, having read the book written about my family, suggested I write one regarding the Downing family. These were friends who had been students at the Rift Valley Academy and had known the Downings and their families.

It took several years for me to decide to contact the Downing children to see if they were amenable to my attempting this task of capturing some of the incredible legacy left by their parents and grandparents, especially as it related to their contribution to RVA.

All the children have been very helpful in providing materials, insights, and recollections. Special thanks to Dottie, Glenn, Ed, Vic, and Lee who mailed me volumes of old letters, diaries, scrapbooks, and pictures; I read many things with interest but had to select only a few.

Thanks also to Phil Dow, whose book *School in the Clouds: The Rift Valley Academy Story,* provided some history. Edith Devitt's *On the Edge of the Rift* painted a picture of what Kijabe was like in the early days. Kenneth Richardson's *Garden of Miracles* and Dick Anderson's *We Felt Like Grasshoppers* also provided helpful information.

For insights into life in the early days and into the Downing family, the unpublished memoirs "My Childhood in Africa" by Lucile Downing Sawhill, and "A Christian Family, Lessons Learned...and the ideal way to learn them" by Gayle Downing Grass were very helpful.

Special thanks go to many former students who wrote me their stories of life at RVA and experiences with the Downings. Most of those have been incorporated in the text. I also talked with several staff members who worked at RVA during the Downing eras who told stories and brought back memories.

Finally, thanks to those who worked hard with little recognition. Esther Shaffer, a good friend and former RVA student, and one who knew the Downing families, read and edited for content. Ed Downing and his wife, Lois, and Dottie Hildebrandt checked out the manuscript for accuracy.

My grateful thanks also to Dave and Gretchen Mills for final editing teamwork with Esther Shaffer, and to Dave for his efforts on text formatting and graphics preparation of the cover and body text. To Jeanne Andersen, who used her artistic skills to provide readers an illustration of the relative placement of buildings at Kijabe mentioned in this book. To granddaughter Heather Snider for using her photographic skills for the author's picture. To David Henry for searching several locations for good pictures of a Cape Chestnut, and to Ted Honer, my good husband who endured, with grace, the mounds of material piled around in his office, and who critiqued my efforts.

For those of us who experienced RVA during those sixty years when the Downings were there, we say thank you to them for helping shape us into what we have become, and for leaving those footprints through the Rift Valley that we can follow with confidence.

Foreword

"Amo, amas, amat;
Amamus, amatus, amant."

This 1934 grade school Latin grammar exercise on "to love," taught by Lee H. Downing, was my introduction to the Downing family. At that time Lee was a very important senior missionary. Yet he had time and heart for this humble task. He set the tone, in my mind, for the ongoing Downing influence at Rift Valley Academy.

Herb and Mildred's arrival at RVA in 1933 brought fresh air in the form of a positive attitude toward students. They had high standards, and they seemed to affirm your ability to achieve those standards, provided you took responsibility.

Herb brought music to life through the orchestra and later the band. Yes, he broadened our horizons in numerous ways. In later years I learned of the expression "Renaissance Man" and realized how well Herb qualified for that title. Herb and Mildred were the very opposite of the RVA faculty caricatured in the novel, *The Quiet Room.*

Mildred was a gifted teacher. But her red hair was a fair warning signal that anything in class that distracted from her imparting her gift was dangerous to the perpetrator. Her class on geography threw wide open the doors of my imagination.

Ken Downing, in his teaching relationships, made me feel that he had walked in my shoes and might himself also have been a "dissident" in some way. He also brought the idea of romance into our thinking. He fell in love with a new missionary nurse from Canada named Ivy Ambrose. Their very evident reciprocal adoration was a charming novelty in that rather Calvinistic mission setting. Ivy practiced nursing in a very pragmatic way. You had to be significantly sick to earn her attention. They were a heaven-made match.

In 1951, my wife, Betty, and I came to RVA as teachers when Herb was principal. In the confused, threatening atmosphere of "Mau Mau," his leadership was serene and sane. Herb spoke the Kikuyu language with greater purity than the majority of Kikuyus under fifty years of age. *Bwana Obaty*, as they called him, enjoyed the enormous trust and love of the Kikuyu people.

In the human tapestry that makes up the story of RVA, few threads are more vivid and more durable than those of the Downing personalities. Each one was an honorable testimony to God's gift of talent and the exercise of it in "applied theology."

Roy D. Shaffer, MD
Albuquerque, New Mexico
2009

Preface

Our first associations with the Downing family happened many years before I was born. It was Africa Inland Mission Field Director Lee H. Downing who graciously accepted my parents, Andrew and Vivian Andersen, into the AIM back in 1913 shortly after they lost almost all they owned in a fire. It was at the Lee Downing home that my brother Earl and sister Lucile were born. In fact, my sister was named Lucile after Lucile Downing.

Lee Downing was my sister Lucile's Latin teacher back when RVA was still a small and "young" school.

After my father died when I was only a toddler, we moved to Kijabe, into the house next door to the Downings. Lee, ever the gracious gentleman, walked with us to church on Sunday afternoons and admonished Mother to make sure her little girls wore sweaters when playing outside. My memories of Lee, by then a widower, are very vague since I was such a little girl, but I do know he was admired in our family.

It was Herbert, then the principal of the school, who listened to Mother when she went to him about her little girl who would not let up nagging that she wanted to go to school. He finally relented and allowed me to start a year early because we were living at Kijabe and I would be a day student. Again, I do not have strong recollections of Herbert and Mildred while I was a very little girl, although I do remember going to their house to find out if my playmates, Gayle and Glenn, could "come out to play."

Herbert and Mildred left for their furlough—which ended up being ten years long—about the time I started school. They returned to RVA just a few months after I left in December 1946, thus being gone all of my school days at RVA.

Kenneth and Ivy stepped in at RVA when Mildred and Herbert left. Kenneth was principal during my nine years and three months tenure as a student at RVA. He and Ivy also served as teachers during that time. More events from my student days at RVA are documented in the book *Missy Fundi: Kenya Girl,* by Mary Andersen Honer.

After completing high school and college I met and married Ted Honer. Together we went to RVA to teach. Now Herbert Downing was the principal and Mildred was a teacher. For two years we served as dormitory supervisors, first for little girls, and then little boys. Since I had two little girls of my own, I did not step right into teaching but took on several interim jobs. One was working in the office. This is where I learned to really appreciate Herbert Downing's work ethic, eclectic and multitudinous abilities, thoughtfulness, and sense of humor. I will always remember the day he glanced up from his desk with an amused look and asked, "I wonder what the kids will do with this name?" A new student was enrolling with the name Christof Puttfarken. Knowing how our students arrived at nicknames that weren't always the most complimentary, we shuddered to think what they might come up with for this one. Fortunately they selected "Putt Putt."

Another day I arrived at the office, now late in my second pregnancy, suggesting I would probably need to cancel my doctor's appointment because of rain and the terrible Kijabe road. Having been through this five times with Mildred, he took one look at me and stated that I was not to break the appointment. In fact, he would see to it that we had some boys to go with us to help in the event of getting stuck in the mud. He was so right: I delivered before the next morning.

We also got to know all the Downing children. Daphne and David were just little tykes when Kenneth and Ivy began their work with RVA. By the time we came on staff, Daphne had gone on to nurse's training, and David, Dottie, Lee, and Vic were in high school and upper elementary grades.

Ruth Ann and Martin were still at home when the Herb Downings were our neighbors at Kijabe. Our girls and Martin were playmates. History was repeating itself. Gayle and Glenn were long since grown up, married, and gone, but later I got to know Tweet (Glenn's wife) when she taught one year at RVA. We never had the privilege of knowing Eddie Lee, as he was called as a kid, until much later when he was an adult. Ed and his wife, Lois, traveled with us to the Centennial celebrations for RVA in 2006.

I guess it can be said that we have a long history with the Downings. What a gifted family! What a pleasure to have known them and to have worked with them in so many capacities and under such varied circumstances. It is indeed a pleasure to have this opportunity to share a little of their legacy with readers as we pay tribute to an amazing family, and especially to their influence on thousands of people scattered around the world.

Map of Kenya
with featured towns and cities underlined

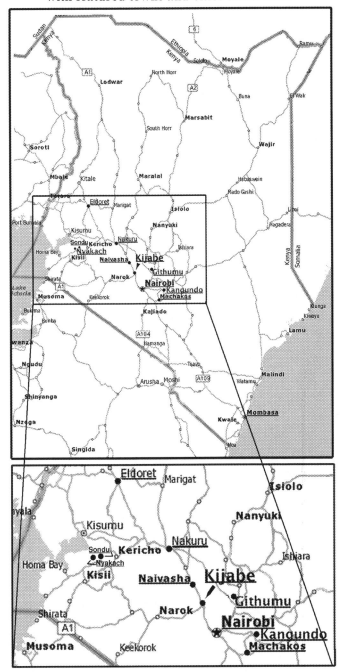

MISS STUMPS HOUSE→

OLD CHURCH BUILDING→

SPORTS
FIELD

SITE OF GYM
17

TENNIS
COURTS

N←

SITE OF CEMETERY

RVA and Kijabe Station

This artist's drawing identifies places mentioned in the text as they related to each other. It is not according to scale and one must recognize that the buildings at the top are hundreds of feet higher in altitude than those below, as Kijabe is built above 7000' on the escarpment of the Great Rift Valley, with forest above, and the plains at 5000' below. Kijabe and RVA have grown into a large community with many new homes and many new dormitories and classrooms. No attempt was made to identify all the structures at Kijabe in this drawing.

Illustration by Jeanne Andersen, 2009

Kijabe Station and RVA Summary Key

Only first occupants of homes are listed below, as many families lived in them over the years, and houses were often used for other purposes. A more complete description of each building is found on the next two pages.

1   **Theodora Hospital**

2   **White Ward**

3   **Doctor's house**

4   **Home of Miss Moody**

5   **Lawson and Chloe Propst home**

6   **AIM office building**

7   **Big red brick house, the home built by Lee Downing**

8   **"Titchie Swot," the nickname of the elementary school**

9   **Original school infirmary**

10   **PTL House**

11   **Henrietta Propst's house**

12   **Rondoval**

13   **One of the Herb Downing homes**

14   **Classroom block housing the Clara Barrett Library**

15   **Jubilee Hall**

16   **RVA (Rift Valley Academy, Kiambogo building)**

17   **Gymnasium site**

18   **Charles and Mae Teasdale house, Moffat Bible School and Kijabe Press.**

19   **Kijabe Hospital**

Kijabe Station and RVA Detailed Key

1. Theodora Hospital. This building was later used as a dormitory for RVA and has since been replaced by a newer dormitory building.
2. The White Ward. This building included a small ward used when missionaries needed maternity or hospital care, housing for nurses upstairs, and an apartment downstairs. It was later used as a dormitory called Stevenson, which burned down in 1959. It was replaced by a new dorm, which later became apartments for staff housing.
3. The doctor's house, later called Twin Gables. Dr. Elwood Davis and then Dr. Jim Propst lived there before it was used for dormitory space. It has been torn down and replaced by two dormitory houses.
4. Originally the home of Miss Moody, one of AIM's earliest missionaries. Now used for staff housing.
5. The Lawson and Chloe Propst home. Grandma Myers, Chloe's widowed mother lived with them. It has since been torn down and water tanks are in its place.
6. The AIM office building shared by Vivian Andersen and her girls after the death of Andrew Andersen. The end room was a *duka* for school supplies for the African school students. The building was later used as a dormitory, and two rooms were added at each end of the long front porch. It has since been turned over to local occupancy.
7. The big red brick house, the home built by Lee Downing soon after they moved to Kijabe. It was later a dormitory but now is no longer used by AIM.
8. "Titchie Swot," the nickname for the elementary school. At one end is an auditorium named Downing Hall. Built later, and not shown, is a library and office addition on the right end.
9. The original school infirmary, and later Coach Dave Reynolds' home. It is currently used as the art building.
10. The PTL House (built by the Pocket Testament League), the home where the Herbert Downings lived just before leaving Kenya.
11. Henrietta Propst's house. Now used for staff housing.

12. The rondoval and small stone house behind (not shown) was Henrietta's mother-in-law, Chloe's home. Then the rondoval was used by Henrietta as a classroom for a while. Later both places were used for staff housing. (The rondoval is currently at Sunrise Acres, Eldama Ravine).
13. Staff housing. One of the Herb Downing homes. Mildred had a classroom built on the side when Martin was a baby so she could be closer to home. It is still used for staff housing.
14. Classroom block with the Clara Barrett Library and several computer labs upstairs. Downstairs are classrooms. At the end is the shop building. Across a courtyard is the science building with classrooms upstairs.
15. Jubilee Hall. This was built and remodeled during Herb Downing's principalship. It has now been replaced by a larger auditorium called Centennial Hall.
16. RVA's Kiambogo Building, whose cornerstone was placed in 1909. This building has gone through several remodelings since the beginning when it housed the whole school—living areas, classrooms, kitchen, office, and all. Now there are offices upstairs and classrooms downstairs. The largest classroom (nicknamed "Big Swot Room") is still used as a staff assembly area for morning prayers and *chai*.
17. The gymnasium occupies this location. It houses a large basketball court, racquetball courts, weight and equipment rooms, and a snack bar and restaurant-type space.
18. The Charles and Mae Teasdale house, Moffat Bible School, and Kijabe Press. This is now all used by Moffat, and the Kijabe Press is in another building farther up the road.
19. Kijabe Hospital. This is a much larger complex than shown.

Below and off to the east of the Downing home was the site of Miss Hulda Stumpf's house, which was torn down after her murder.

Well off the page and below the big brick house was the old African Church. It has now been replaced by a much larger building.

The Kijabe Cemetery is below the hospital. This is where Ken and Ivy are buried as well as many others mentioned in the text.

1.

Beginnings

Lee Harper Downing

The young professor trudged along the path, satchel in hand and deep in thought. He was a small man, maybe five foot seven or eight, and very slight of build with large piercing blue eyes. His hair was thin and fine making his ears appear to protrude even more than usual. Right now his mind kept returning to the young lady in one of his classes who had grabbed more than her share of his attention. He wondered how he could approach her while his mind whirled with the urgings and call he was feeling toward mission work. As he walked along, his mind kept shifting between concern and prayer, contemplating life and his future.

Teaching Latin and Greek at the Philadelphia Bible Institute should be rewarding enough without the constant nagging he endured that perhaps God might want him to serve overseas. If he were to choose that route, what should or could he do about the young lady in his class who seemed to occupy more and more of his thoughts? Was it fair to ask Blanche to marry him and to go to a country full of danger, poor living conditions and disease, a place where life expectancy was so short? As he always did, he made all his troubling thoughts a matter of prayer and rested in the knowledge that his Heavenly Father knew best and would work out His plan for his life.

Reaching his room, he climbed the stairs and found the key to his door. Inside he dropped the satchel on the floor and sat down at the desk. Strewn over the desk were pamphlets, letters, notes from sermons, and lectures, all regarding a relatively new work in Kenya, British East Africa, under an organization called Africa Inland Mission.

Lee picked up one of the brochures and reread the information about the group who went to Kenya under the leadership of Peter Cameron Scott, a young Scotsman, who had initially gone to the

Congo on the west coast of Africa. After two years in Congo, during which he suffered repeated bouts of fever, Peter had determined he would approach Africa from the east. With a small group of men and women, he sailed for Mombasa in August 1895 and proceeded inland to establish the first Africa Inland Mission station. Unfortunately, his body had already been compromised by recurring fevers, and within two years he was dead from black water fever, a complication of the dreaded malaria. Three others of the initial group also died, and three more returned home broken in body. Only one was able to stay in Africa.

However, by 1896, Peter's parents had already led the second wave of missionaries out to the field, and a third wave was being prayerfully assembled by Rev. Charles Hurlburt, president of the Philadelphia Bible Institute. As Lee read and thought about these early pioneers, he visualized the unbelievable pain of leaving loved ones, the likely possibility of succumbing to malaria or some other deadly disease. Could he expect or even ask Blanche to consider going with him? Travel was long and arduous by ship, sometimes taking months to reach their destination. When one got letters, which were few and far between, it often took six months for a response to a question.

With the assurance that God was indeed calling him to foreign service, and since he truly loved this young lady, Lee committed the situation to his Heavenly Father. If it was His will, Blanche would agree to be his wife and follow him to the ends of the earth. If not, he would have to deal with that later. Now it was time to ask her.

2.

Lee and Blanche Downing

Lee Harper Downing

Lee Harper was born June 28, 1866, in Lloydsville, Belmont County, Ohio. He had one older brother, John Alexander, who was born April 16, 1865. These two boys were born to Margaret Ann Harper, who was Alexander Downing's second wife. Margaret was considerably younger than Alexander, having been born the same year as William, Alexander's son by his first wife.

Alexander Downing was a big man, standing at six foot, four inches tall. Margaret was almost six feet tall, and older brother Alexander was over six feet tall. Lee was five feet seven inches and slight in build, weighing only about 130 pounds. Perhaps because he was so thin, his ears seemed too large for his head, which earned him the nickname "Rabbit Ears." While he did not enjoy brawn, he did excel intellectually, using his keen mind to memorize and retain easily, which helped him with his studies in math and languages.

Unfortunately, Alexander Sr. died when Lee was just six years old, and Lee had no memory of his father. His mother died when he was ten. All his life Lee suffered from asthma and struggled for breath. His most vivid memory of his mother was of having her hold him up so that he could breathe better.

After their parents' death, the two little boys were placed in several different foster homes. The couple that was most influential, and who became their legal guardians, was Famie and John Caldwell. Here the two boys found a loving home and soon felt as though these people were their parents. Famie died while Lee was in college, and John Caldwell remarried a woman by the name of Grizella. The tone of the household quickly changed as this lady, nicknamed Griz, was a hard-working, taciturn, unbending, super-conservative United Presbyterian who thought it a sin to even re-warm coffee or make a meal on the Sabbath. Only Psalms were to be sung, and it seemed that Old Testament law was re-instituted each week in the house. The family soon learned what it meant to live "under the law."

Having been left a small inheritance by his parents and wanting a college education, Lee had enrolled at Franklin College in New Athens, Ohio. (This college was later absorbed by Muskingum College.) He completed his formal education at Washington and Jefferson College, Washington, Pennsylvania, in 1892, with highest honors and as valedictorian of his class.

In the meantime his brother, Alexander, who was always fascinated by trains and the railroad as a child, left the farm at age sixteen and went to work for the Baltimore and Ohio Railway, with which he remained until his death in 1928. As a little boy he could identify engines by the sound of their whistles, and he read all he could about these huge locomotives. Having a job with the railway was a fulfillment of his fondest dreams.

Lee Downing

Unlike his brother, Lee was more academic and cerebral in his interests and gifts. After his graduation from Jefferson College, Lee got a teaching position at Philadelphia Bible School, where he was professor of Latin and New Testament Greek and where he led studies in the epistles. In 1899, he served as secretary and treasurer of the Philadelphia Missionary Council. Here he became acquainted with Charles Hurlburt and the fledgling group later known as Africa Inland Mission. This move was to change his life and open horizons he never could have anticipated in his wildest dreams.

Blanche Hunter Downing

Blanche Hunter was born in McArthur, Vinton County, Ohio, on September 28, 1872. She was the daughter of George Hunter and Marietta Hoffhine. The Hunters were Scotch-Irish, and the Hoffhines were German. Grandfather Hoffhine was a "real martinet" by reputation and ran a "very tight ship." Blanche's mother, Marietta, was a daughter by George's first wife, Maria.

When Blanche was ten years old, her mother died of tuberculosis, leaving three children: Carl, age twelve; Blanche, ten; and Herbert, eight. These three were shunted around among the relatives until deemed able to fend for themselves, which happened when they were still very young. Aunt Lizzie, whom the Downing children often visited, was the daughter of George's second wife.

Their father's second marriage had failed to make life easier, as the stepmother exemplified the picture portrayed in the story of Cinderella. For several happy years Blanche was able to escape and lived in the home of one of her father's sisters, Axie Winters. Although Aunt Axie

Blanche Hunter Downing

had a large family of her own, she made room for another in her heart and home.

In her late twenties Blanche enrolled in the Philadelphia Bible Institute as a student. There she soon attracted the attention of the New Testament Greek and Latin professor. Looking at this thin young man, Blanche thought, *If I cooked for you, I could fatten you up.* Lee, on the other hand, although attracted, felt that Blanche's blouses were inappropriate. He never would tell his children or grandchildren whether they were too sheer, too tight, or had a neckline that revealed too much in his estimation. However, he seemed able to overlook this minor problem and to appreciate the lovely girl hidden under the questionable middy blouse.

Sometime during her two years at PBI, Lee felt the call to mission work and settled in his mind to follow the pioneers and the mission established by Peter Cameron Scott. Blanche surely knew about the Africa Inland Mission, as the Pennsylvania Bible Institute had played such a leading role in the training and formation of the mission. Would Blanche consider going with him?

Blanche's brother judged his sister to be very particular and picky when it came to men. When she had spurned several suitors, her brother Carl commented, "Anyone she'd ever marry would have to be gilt-edged." It was with anticipation and curiosity therefore, that he learned that Blanche had accepted the proposal of Professor Lee Downing.

In his practical and methodical way, Lee had carefully outlined his plan to go to Africa under Africa Inland Mission, which was a faith mission, meaning they probably would not have money. He told Blanche that she might not have a nice home, the climate was problematic for foreigners, and he really did not know what difficulties they might face. However, he did love her and felt that God had placed this love in his heart for her, and he wanted her to consider his marriage proposal in light of the information he had given her.

We do not know if Blanche responded immediately, or if she took some time to think. However, on October 10, 1899, they were married in the home of her brother Carl's wife's family. October had been chosen because Lee suffered seriously with asthma during the spring and summer seasons. There were no flower decorations or bouquets in consideration of Lee's allergies, and her wedding dress was undoubtedly rather simple and practical. Rather than flowers, Blanche carried a linen handkerchief. (That handkerchief was also carried by her daughter Lucile and her granddaughter Phyllis and perhaps will go on down the line.) Blanche had no money and Lee very little as they embarked on this journey of marriage. Since rings were not obligatory, Blanche did not receive a wedding ring. Many years later she was able to save enough from her butter and eggs money to buy a gold band. In Kenya, English women wore rings, and Blanche felt that she was looked at with curiosity and questions since her finger was bare. Her hints to Lee about getting a ring went unheeded, so she bought her own.

Brother Carl, who had waited to see what kind of a man Blanche would settle for, appraised Lee and made the comment to his sister, "You have indeed picked a gilt-edged man." Until the wedding, the family had not met Lee, but their appraisal and approval was immediate.

Two years later, in October 1901, Lee and Blanche Downing sailed away from Philadelphia bound for Africa with the third wave of AIM missionaries to go to work on "The Dark Continent," led by Charles Hurlburt.

3.

British East Africa

Philadelphia was the port from which much of Africa Inland Mission launched in its early days. As a professor at the Philadelphia Bible Institute, Lee had many opportunities to hear people such as Charles Hurlburt speak about his vision for British East Africa. He must have listened to Peter Cameron Scott, who took the first AIM group out in 1895, the same year Hurlburt had established PBI. With others like Scott who were interested in Africa, Hurlburt had formed the Philadelphia Missionary Council to bolster AIM's efforts. This council attracted Lee. He soon found himself secretary and treasurer of it and interested enough to join the small band preparing to go to the mission field.

The second AIM group had already left: Mr. and Mrs. John Scott, who were Peter's parents; Ina Scott, his sister; and Willis Hotchkiss sailed for British East Africa in June 1896.

Charles Hurlburt and his Philadelphia Missionary Council were working on the constitution for the Africa Inland Mission. He was adamant that AIM would adhere strictly to a faith basis for the raising of funds. No one would be given a salary, and all would solely depend on God's supplying all their needs. There was much discussion pro and con, but Hurlburt finally triumphed and the policy was set. With some modifications, the principle of full information regarding the work, but no solicitation for funds, won out. After giving over his position as director of the Bible institute to a superintendent, Hurlburt had seen his faith tested and strengthened. Immediately upon taking office, the new man had begun to solicit funds. The institute nearly went bankrupt, but when the faith basis was reinstated, the institute prospered, which Hurlburt took as God's reassurance that the faith basis was right and confirmed to him that God was leading.

Lee and Blanche joined the group who left New York in October 1901 and reached Mombasa on December 11. In this party were Charles Hurlburt, his wife Alta, their five children, Emily Messenger, and Dr. John Henderson. God honored Charles Hurlburt, who was a man of prayer and vision, with strength and health enough to remain many years in Africa. He served as general director of AIM until

1926. God used all five of his children in mission service in later years.

When they reached Mombasa, the Downings found that the Uganda Railway had been built to within miles of Nairobi. Doubtless they were told the stories of the man-eating lions encountered in the building of this railway. They traveled through territory soon made famous by J. H. Patterson's 1907 book, *The Man-Eaters of Tsavo*. When one reads this book and realizes the hazards experienced by the many men building it, the railway stands as a marvel to the tenacity of the pioneering spirit in opening up East Africa. Hence it was dubbed "The Lunatic Express." Many died of disease, while others were dragged away by lions, making the railway an expensive feat of engineering skill and human sacrifice.

The Downings traveled to the end of the rail line, which at that time was the Athi River station. From there they walked or rode donkeys to Kangundo, where a mission station had been started by those earliest pioneers. Machakos was the closest trading post for Ukambaland, thus called because the local people spoke Kikamba. After loading their possessions on porters and donkeys, they headed for Kangundo, which was to be their new home.

Although the distance between the rail line and Kangundo was not long, the half-day trip seemed endless. The young missionaries, already tired from the slow and arduous train ride, now were jounced about on hot, smelly, and stubborn donkeys. The hot equatorial sun beat down mercilessly, and the flies and insects were a constant nuisance. Since the average speed was slow and slower, the riders sometimes got off to walk ahead, where they waited under a tree until the rest caught up to them. Their new home was a welcome sight, even if it was only made of sun-dried bricks and had a thatched roof.

***

At Kangundo, on November 25, 1902, Lucile was born. She was the first white baby born in the area and so immediately became the object of much curiosity among the local people. Many walked miles just to see this unusual phenomenon and to reassure themselves that white people were really born that color and didn't bleach out later.

Lee had been anxious to have a child and made it clear that he truly wanted a little daughter. He was delighted with this addition to his family and was demonstratively affectionate with his baby daughter, using the term "Pettie" as his name of endearment.

The Akamba people held one of the customs that disconcerted many mothers in the early days. Their form of blessing or cursing was to spit. To bless, the saliva was gently sprayed through slightly parted lips. The curse came through the two front teeth with as much force as the ejector could produce. The Akamba used to file the front teeth into little points, leaving a space large enough to expel a large gob of spit. This custom of filing teeth came from the days when lockjaw was prevalent and the sick person needed to be fed through clenched jaws. Now that spacing between teeth was used with great efficiency to curse.

Needless to say, European (as all white people were identified) mothers were repulsed by having their babies spat upon, even though the spitter was sending a shower of blessing. Blanche Downing was no exception and found it unacceptable to have her little girl spat upon. Rather than cause an incident, a compromise was reached. The admirers muttered a blessing and then spat on the ground. One wonders if they added a few words to the blessing, but most missionaries would not have known the language well enough to recognize any disparaging remarks.

Right along with learning English at home, Lucile soon learned to converse with the local people and from them learned that being white was not the reason the European was admired. It was the perceived wealth and possessions of the white man that caused the admiration, although his skill and ingenuity was also admired. However, among the Africans, having white skin was not considered a desirable attribute because it burned in the sun and became red and splotchy. They noticed that most of the white people wore long sleeves, long pants, and pith or felt hats with wide brims despite the temperatures and blazing sun, while the Africans had little covering and were exposed to any fresh breeze that happened to come along. As Lucile grew up she thought she detected that most Africans preferred brunettes to blondes.

***

Kangundo was a real learning experience for Blanche and stretched her ability to adjust and adapt. Keeping the Africans from blessing her baby by spitting on her was only one of a multitude of hurdles. The constant buzzing of flies during the day and mosquitoes at night were enough to drive her crazy.

Their house was made of sun-dried bricks with large, overhanging eaves. This was done to prevent the walls from washing away in a heavy rain and also to provide some shade and shelter from the hot midday sun. The house only had two rooms: a living room and a bedroom. The kitchen was located outside in a separate hut. The floor was hard-packed earth, and the few windows were covered with unbleached muslin that let in light but also prevented one from looking out. Shutters were used during rains or when the weather was cold. There was a wooden door made with planks held together by a crossbar at the top and bottom, with a diagonal between the two making a large Z pattern. Earliest houses had thatched roofs, as did the African houses.

Since missionaries did not build fires in their home in the middle of the floor so that the smoke would keep rodents, bugs, and snakes away as in the African houses, people like the Downings hung unbleached muslin across the rafters to catch droppings and prevent creatures from falling into food or onto furniture below. This unbleached muslin that missionaries used for so many purposes was commonly known among the Europeans as "Americana," or *americani* in Swahili. Many Africans were clothed in a *shuka,* a length of *americani* tied on one shoulder toga-style, often with a second one tied on the other shoulder. A higher grade of muslin and closer weave was called *maridufu.*

In his book, *The Hotchkiss Luck,* Willis L. Hotchkiss (son of an early missionary with AIM) writes about Americana: "Years later, I heard the story that in the last days of the American Civil War an American merchant ship carrying a huge stock of the muslin had dropped anchor at Mombasa harbor and had done a thriving and profitable business in exchanging the muslin for ivory, exotic hides of lions, leopards, zebras and the like. The muslin became so popular that it then and thereafter was called Americana."

But in Blanche's outside kitchen built like an African hut, the *americani* was not used for a ceiling. It probably would have caught fire anyway, as much of the cooking was done over an open fire on three stones. It was only after one of her furloughs that Blanche was able to return to Kenya with a big black wood-burning stove with a hot water tank attached. This seemed like real luxury!

Lucile related an incident that happened during the pre-stove era that illustrates why the *americani* ceilings were felt to be important. Being largely vegetarian, the Akamba usually didn't butcher meat to eat. They waited until an animal became sick, was about to die, and was definitely of no further use, before it was put out of its misery and the people had meat to eat. For some strange reason the missionaries did not cotton to this custom too well. On one occasion a goat was accidentally killed, and the missionaries were able to negotiate the purchase of meat from an animal that had not been sick. Blanche brewed up a big stew in the kitchen and invited guests for dinner. With all the missionaries on the station gathered for this celebration, Blanche went to the kitchen to serve the stew. At that exact, but inappropriate, moment, a rat fell from the ceiling and dropped into the stew. The African cook extracted the rat, but Blanche insisted that the stew be brought back to a boil and left there for several minutes. The stew was served and enjoyed by all, except Blanche, whose lack of appetite she quietly attributed to fatigue!

Blanche found that her idea of sanitation and that of the Africans often did not agree. She had a difficult time instilling the need for cleanliness into the cooks she tried to train. One day, her cook had a difficult time understanding why she objected when she observed him alternating between turning pancakes and scratching his bare leg with the same spatula.

The blowing of the nose was another problem for the early missionary. Since handkerchiefs or tissues were not available, the local people used their thumb and forefinger. The snot was then flicked off onto the ground, and if necessary the hand was wiped on leaves or grass. Washing the hand was not considered necessary.

There was the constant battle with flies. Without screens on the windows and doors it was impossible to keep flies off the food. Africans were so used to flies in their eyes, on their mouths, and all over their food, that it was hard for them to understand the constant waving of hands to discourage the flies landing on a plate of food. Necessity being the mother of invention, jug covers came into being and were widely used by early missionaries. These were circles of netting, usually doubled and weighted down by designs of beading around the edges. Most people had varying sizes to fit the different pitchers (commonly called jugs) and serving dishes at the table. Some missionaries and their children created rather fancy beadwork and made the jug covers a work of art.

For a lady who enjoyed pretty and feminine things and insisted on cleanliness, the adjustment to these primitive conditions did not come easily for Blanche. However, she tried to make her little house homey and as clean as possible. Enjoying her little girl, Lucile, and being married to a good husband, Lee, made life tolerable, although there were days and nights she longed for a nice house and the amenities of life in the United States.

***

In 1905 the Downings moved from Kangundo to Kijabe. Initially the house they moved into was very much like the one they had in Kangundo with the exception that this one had four rooms, a *mabati* (corrugated iron) roof and glass windows. The floor was still dirt and the ceilings *americani*. Although this house was a step up, it was far from Blanche's dream house. At least this time she had windows she could dress with curtains, and the whole family did not have to share the same bedroom.

Blanche now found that her ideas of a woman's place were somewhat different than those of many of her fellow women missionaries. For most the work was primary, but for Blanche her family came first. Although she had several lady friends, she was not particularly popular, especially among those who held with their idea of a missionary calling.

Probably because of her views, she was looked on as arrogant and outspoken. For her children it meant that they knew they came before the "work." In their minds there was never a question of taking second place to missionary service.

This did not mean that Blanche was uninvolved in the greater work. With a husband who served as Treasurer and later Field Director, she had more than her share of hosting. Missionaries coming to Kijabe to deliver babies or with other medical problems often stayed with the Downings before and after the birth or until they were able to return to their more remote locations. Others, on a journey up or down country, stopped en route for a bath, bed, and good food. With these guests Blanche was warm and welcoming, but they certainly added to the workload.

She also worked with some of the African women, teaching them to sew. Since she was a perfectionist, the work had to be done correctly, no matter the number of times it was necessary to rip something out and do it again. One African woman stitched so well that it was difficult to distinguish her sewing from that of a sewing machine. Lucile recalled learning to darn socks. The darning must be perfectly woven, or else it was ripped out and done again. Since both parents were perfectionists, Lucile wondered how she managed to get into that family!

Blanche's heart was heavy for the African women. They were treated as property and burdened with all the heavy work of building houses, hoeing the garden, cooking, and bearing children. It was the women who cut and carried immense bundles of firewood on their backs, pots of water on their heads, and perhaps a baby tied atop the wood.

Because of her concern for these women, Blanche began holding a tea party for them after sewing class. Although there was a definite language barrier since Blanche never learned Kikuyu well, it was here she began to absorb some of the lessons of the culture. Lucile recalled one of those instances.

Blanche baked a whole batch of cookies in anticipation of serving her women something good after their efforts at sewing. She carefully stacked the cookies on the plate and passed them around the group. Since her Kikuyu was limited, all her communication attempts were made with the use of motions and grunts with a word or two thrown in. The women happily ate the delicious sweets and helped themselves to seconds and thirds until the whole batch of cookies was finished. Blanche learned that according to Kikuyu custom, it was impolite to stop eating until all the food offered was finished. From then on she only placed on the plate what she wanted eaten.

Around these sewing lessons and tea parties came some interesting conversations. Despite the language barrier, Blanche managed to communicate with these women. One of the topics explored was the difference in husbands. The African women could not understand love as defined by the white person. The African man expressed his caring by offering a larger bride price. If he really "loved" a girl he was willing to pay more cows. How could it be said that a white man loved a woman for whom he had paid nothing?

On the other hand Blanche struggled with the concept of sharing the man she loved with several other wives. The African women seemed to take the idea of second and third wives as common practice and therefore acceptable. However, Blanche had to agree that sharing some of the wifely duties and household chores with some other women wasn't all bad!

***

Being a scholar, Lee soon learned Kikuyu and even helped put the language into writing. His ability with Latin and Greek and good knowledge of Hebrew undoubtedly helped in this endeavor. He was fascinated by words and enjoyed the study of pronunciation, derivations, and especially the shades of meaning. He was a stickler for correct grammar (a trait passed on to his children and ultimately to those of us who attended RVA).

His mission duties as field director resulted in Lee's being away from home often. Blanche was left with the responsibility of disciplining the children. When he was home Lee did his share. He was a strict disciplinarian, expecting obedience, respect, and honesty. Even though he was slight of build, he had big hands and a powerful arm. Although he did not spank often, when he did, it was memorable.

4.

First Furlough

Lucile was two and a half years old when the Downings moved from Kangundo to Kijabe. It was there on August 14, 1905, that Lee and Blanche welcomed a baby boy, Herbert Caldwell Downing. Before he was a year old, Herbert and his family sailed across the Atlantic Ocean to America.

Blanche had never been very strong and healthy, and the stress of life in East Africa did not help. Lee, on the other hand, was thriving and had been given more and more responsibility in Africa Inland Mission. Blanche needed medical attention that she could not get in Kenya, but it was felt that Lee could not be spared to leave Kenya at that time. So, with a rambunctious three-year-old Lucile and a six-month-old Herbert, Blanche set off on the long voyage home. The three left Kijabe on February 7 and reached New York on April 7, 1906.

Besides not being well in the first place, now Blanche struggled with seasickness. Throwing up, nursing a baby, and watching three-year-old Lucile were more than she could handle. Fortunately, several of the ladies aboard came to the rescue and offered to entertain Lucile, thus giving Blanche some respite, though she still had the needs of the baby and her own illness with which to contend.

Despite her best efforts, one day Blanche realized that Lucile was nowhere to be found. She searched with increasing anxiety until she found Lucile perched up on a table in the salon entertaining a group of German men. The men were plying Lucile with sips of beer while she entertained them by singing hymns in Kikuyu. Blanche was mortified and angrily removed her daughter from the table and off to their cabin.

Being on a German ship and knowing no German did not help the situation. Crossing the Atlantic was miserable, and Blanche was unable to keep any food down. One day the smell of sauerkraut and the thought of that savory dish sounded wonderful. She ordered some, and the steward, believing that this would not sit well, only brought a small portion. For some reason this German specialty tasted good, and the hungry Blanche looked disappointed at the size of her portion. Her table companions suggested she order *saur kraut sehr veil.* This brought a platter heaped up with sauerkraut. The results of this indulgence were not reported, but New York was a welcome sight to this beleaguered lady and her two children.

When Blanche had recovered from the trip and the undisclosed medical problem was taken care of, she began to do the furlough circuit of visiting friends, family, and supporters. One of the stops was at the home of Lucile's uncle Carl, aunt Stella, and cousins Ruth and Robert, who lived in the South. The two American children were discussing what they would do with their little African cousins when they arrived. Of course they would take their cousins to Sunday School, but what would their classmates think of having black children visit?

Lucile recounted that she still recalled that Sunday School session. Fortunately she did not elicit curiosity because of her color, but she became the one who was curious. The class was celebrating Memorial Day and singing patriotic songs. They sang "Three Cheers for the Red, White, and Blue." But who were Red, White, and Blue, and why did they need chairs? After much puzzlement over the following days she decided it must have been American names for Father, Son, and Holy Ghost! She never did decide what "Columbia, the Gem of the Ocean" was all about but didn't bother to ask anyone.

Meanwhile, back in Kenya, Lee had been fulfilling his roles, first as corresponding secretary for the mission and then as treasurer.

Lee finally decided he needed to join the family in the United States, leaving Kenya March 2 and arriving in New York on April 7, 1907. On December 3, 1907, Lee, Blanche, Lucile, and Herbert returned to Kenya and Kijabe. Blanche had another miserable voyage with the added nausea caused by a new pregnancy. At least this time she had a husband to help her with the children.

5.

Kijabe

After living in the little four-room house at Kijabe with the dirt floors for a time, Lee decided he needed to do something about more comfortable accommodations for his growing family. Blanche was expecting their third child in June, and it was December. He needed to get busy quickly.

He had received an inheritance and still had some left with which he wanted to build Blanche a house she could decorate and make comfortable, a true home for his children. He selected a site on the hillside with a marvelous view of the Great Rift Valley. Being on a hillside

The Big Red Brick house

meant some excavation in order to make a place flat enough on which to build. With the red earth that was dug out he made bricks, which were fired in a kiln he constructed.

The house had four equal-sized rooms downstairs and four upstairs. The walls were eighteen inches thick, and this time Blanche would have real windows ordered from Montgomery Ward. Until the order arrived six months later, *americani* was used to keep out the prying eyes. It was during this time that a nocturnal visit was made by a leopard that strolled through the house after finding an open door that created easy access off the back porch. Since Lee was away, Lucile was sleeping with her mother. The doors to the hallway were closed and locked, but the windows and access to the upstairs back porch were available. Initially, Lucile and Blanche attributed the noise to a neighbor's large dog. But when they heard the visitor jump from the landing on the stairs down to the bottom floor, they suspected it to be a large cat. The animal came back up the stairs, and then went out the back door, off the porch onto the hillside, and back into the forest.

In the morning when the cook came to work, he excitedly reported finding muddy footprints all around the house and up the stairs. He knew them to be those of a large leopard. Blanche and Lucile became more vigilant about locking the outside door. And they were very glad when the glass windows arrived from Montgomery Ward.

On the first floor of the big brick house were a living room, a dining room, and a study with a separate outside door so that people could come to the office without going through the house. The fourth room was a kitchen with pantry. The kitchen also had an outside door to facilitate the African help and people coming house to house selling vegetables and eggs.

Upstairs were four rooms and an addition on the back that housed a bathtub and washstand for a basin and water jug. Without a sewer and indoor plumbing, one had to make a trek outside and up the hill to the outhouse. Around this little outhouse Lee built a trellis for Blanche's sweet peas that helped to hide its presence and also added some more pleasant fragrance. Inside, old Montgomery Ward and Sears catalogs provided browsing and reading materials and sometimes even served as toilet paper, as that was a luxury hard to come by.

At the front door a small covered porch was constructed, somewhat breaking the look of a square brick box. Blanche planted a beautiful yellow climbing rose that made its way up and over the top of this porch, creating a welcoming arbor. Her green thumb, especially for roses, became legendary. A circular drive leading to the house was made, and in the circle some fruit trees were planted.

**Friends and neighbors visit the Downings on the front steps
of the big brick house.**

With the construction of the sawmill at Kijabe, it was possible to get boards to make the floors. No more hard-packed earth floors! Blanche was thrilled, despite the wagging tongues. There was criticism for spending God's money for this big house. Others thought it unwise to build a two-storied house in Africa, especially at this altitude where one had to consider one's heart and lungs. However, since the house was located on a small piece of land carved out of the hillside, it needed to sit on a smaller base. Let the tongues wag; Lee went right ahead with his creation.

Lee, who was a perfectionist, made built-in cupboards and storage compartments using his hand tools and any other means available. The wood used for the office floor smelled peppery and was some sort of very hard wood, making it almost unworkable, so Lee chose softer wood for the rest of the floors and woodwork.

Blanche had acquired a few pieces of furniture that she brought back with her from furlough. Some of their furnishings were bought from other missionaries leaving the country for good. Other furniture was borrowed while their owners were away on furlough. It was in this way that a piano and organ came to live in the Downing house.

Lee brought to Kenya his "spool" bed that had been his as a boy when living on the Caldwell farm.

With Blanche's gift for gardening, the yard was soon verdant with flowers and fruit trees. Lemon, loquat, and custard apple were among the different fruits. Roses were a specialty, with all sorts of colors and sizes. On the far side of the house, a vegetable garden provided beautiful carrots, rhubarb, cabbages, and many other crops. The rich virgin soil yielded wonderful produce. Of course there was always the problem of rabbits and small antelope who enjoyed the tasty treats.

***

Kenneth Lee Downing was born on June 26, 1908, in the big brick house at Kijabe. Lucile and Herbert were in the other room waiting to hear whether they got a brother or sister. Blanche reported that when Herbert heard the first cries, he began to sing "The Fight Is On, O Christian Soldiers." Lucile didn't recall that incident but did recall the disappointment she and Herbert felt when they met their new brother. "He was so red, and wrinkled, and squirmy, and he wouldn't even look at us!"

A stable provided a place for a pony named Billy and for calves that perhaps needed extra care away from the herd. This area was designated as Herbert's responsibility. Blanche also had chickens that were her pride and joy. She was convinced that her flock of buff Orpington chickens would provide the best eggs. As soon as he was old enough, feeding the chickens and gathering the eggs became Kenneth's responsibility. Lucile had the task of helping with household chores. The one she hated most was cleaning the glass chimneys of the kerosene lanterns. Unless the wicks were trimmed exactly right, or if someone turned them up too high, they smoked and created a black sludge on the chimney. Carefully filling the lanterns with kerosene was a chore fraught with its own problems for Lucile's little hands. Although she used a funnel, it was impossible to know exactly how full the tank was until the liquid began backing up into the funnel. Then taking the funnel out could make kerosene spill, causing a terrible smell and possible damage to what lay beneath. Choosing a good location for this delicate operation was important.

Although there were probably only six to eight lanterns, it felt like a hundred to Lucile.

At one time the boys had the care and feeding of a couple of small oxen. Since an ox cart was the common mode of transportation, Herb and Ken decided to build themselves an ox cart. They constructed a box on which they attached wheels and then made a tongue and yoke for the little oxen. This task provided many hours of work and pleasure until the oxen became too big for play and the boys had to look for other amusements. They tried using a calf and a goat to pull their cart with limited success.

Between the stable and the house was built a brick oven in which bread could

Herb and Ken build their own ox cart, here drawn by a calf and a goat.

be baked. One could not run to the store to buy a loaf of bread. It had to be made by hand, and, with three growing children and lots of company, the Downings kept the ovens busy. Blanche trained an African how to build the fire and to make sure it burned down to just the right amount of coals and correct temperature. This was all done by feel and intuition. After the hot coals were scraped out, the risen loaves were placed in the oven and the heavily insulated door put into place. The cook learned how to tap the loaves for the correct sound of doneness after an appropriate baking time. Sometimes they needed to be turned out of the pan and replaced upside-down for a few minutes to insure the inside was baked. It was amazing how these African men learned to make marvelous bread and other foreign dishes, considering that making bread and cooking *mzungu* foods was new for them.

Down the hill a short distance a larger vegetable garden was planted for potatoes, corn, and other crops needing more space. Kijabe had an ideal climate for growing since the temperatures were mild and on good years the rain was adequate. Wild animals, big and small, were a problem for both the vegetable gardens and the domestic animals. Leopards liked making a meal of the chickens and calves and any pets. Mongooses loved the chickens and their eggs, and they seemed capable of getting through the smallest opening to wreak their havoc. Monkeys, antelope, and rabbits enjoyed the vegetables, so, although things grew well, the harvest sometimes was meager.

Also down the hill, Lee planted low-growing evergreens that seemed to be configured into a sort of maze. When the trees were large enough, he trimmed them so they blocked out the view of passersby. In the center he often went to pray when some burden became heavy.

With continuing responsibilities being added and the mission constantly growing, Lee felt the need to retreat to his secret place more often. He had already served as corresponding secretary, then treasurer, and finally field director. Blanche found herself doing more and more entertaining as guests came through Kijabe. The Downing house was a busy place.

***

Getting mail from home was a lifeline that many missionaries clung to for survival. Mail days were anticipated, and when nothing came, the disappointment was palpable. Mail to Kijabe was routed through Mombasa, the only port of entrance to Kenya, and on into Uganda and Congo. Letters were addressed, "Kijabe, via Mombasa."

From Mombasa the mail was sent on the train to Kijabe, where it had to be picked up at the railway station three miles down the hill from the mission compound. For this job a young Kikuyu man was hired named Karanja wa Kago. Faithfully for many years he trekked up and down those hills through rain and leopard-inhabited forest to pick up and deliver mail for the missionaries. In the October 1917 issue of *Inland Africa*, which was the mission magazine, there appeared an account of Karanja's wedding to Njeri wa Kiai, who attended the Kijabe Girls School. Theirs was a June wedding at the little church at Kijabe. Karanja being somewhat a celebrity at Kijabe, his wedding was well attended by both black and white people. This was a Christian wedding, but some of the African cultural customs were observed. Njeri, who lived in the Girls' Home at Kijabe, was not to appear anxious or in a hurry to enter into this marriage. She therefore took her time getting to the church. After reaching the church door, she had to be encouraged to come in and eventually helped by one of the missionaries down the aisle. Although all her attendants were whites, and the wedding banns had been published and announced the mandatory three weeks prior, Njeri played out her native custom of reticence and bashfulness to the hilt.

Lucile Downing played Wagner's "Wedding March" from Lohengrin as the bride came down the aisle attended by her missionary bridesmaid. The church had been decorated with white Calla lilies and ferns. (Although not reported in the article, the bride probably carried marigolds, as the African girls found those the flower of choice for their bouquet.) The service ended with the singing of "Love Divine, All Loves Excelling," as translated into Kikuyu. Refreshments were served at the Girls' Home, and toward evening, also according to custom, the newlyweds were accompanied to their home by the girl's friends living at the Home.

This was an atypical wedding, especially in those early years. So many couples followed tribal customs and were married "heathen" style. Some were then remarried in the church after conversion. Having one of the school girls and a favorite mailman married for the first time in a Christian wedding was indeed newsworthy.

Karanja must have kept that job for over thirty years and faithfully delivered the mail, even though as the years went by and more people came to Kijabe, the bags of letters became heavier. He walked those three miles down and back up every day. Most missionaries suspect he will certainly be granted God's blessing of "Well done, thou good and faithful servant."

6.

Rift Valley Academy, 1906–1933

Recognizing that missionaries' children needed an education, Charles Hurlburt asked Josephine Hope, a new young missionary, to consider using her skills as a Montessori teacher to educate the four of them that were at Kijabe at that time. Although she had intended to use her skills for the local population, she agreed to take on the task. At first her classroom was in one side of a mud-and-wattle building shared by a class of African students on the other side. The first classes of the Rift Valley Academy were started in 1906.

By 1909, money had been donated by a gentleman in memory of his stepmother, a Mrs. Butterworth, to be used to erect a school for missionaries' children. In 1908, the building was begun in time for a visit from Theodore Roosevelt, the former American president, who was in Kenya on a hunting safari. While on a furlough, Hurlburt had been summoned to the White House to meet with Theodore

Kiambogo building

Roosevelt because the president wanted to know about Kenya and hunting opportunities, thus establishing an acquaintance and a deep respect for each other. So when Hurlburt learned that President Roosevelt would be in Kenya, he asked if Roosevelt would do the honor of placing the cornerstone for this American school in the heart of Africa. Roosevelt agreed, and the Kijabe mission people began preparations.

A potluck dinner was arranged so that all the missionaries could greet and welcome Mr. Roosevelt. This was definitely a very special occasion and called for whatever the little community of Kijabe

Cornerstone laid by President Theodore Roosevelt August 4, 1909

managed to produce. Chloe Myers Propst wrote: "We made a large American flag for the occasion. Mrs. Westervelt dyed unbleached muslin red and blue, and figured the proportions of the different sections. I sewed the 'stars and stripes' together..."

The building, called Kiambogo, still stands with the cornerstone placed by the former president in place. A plaque remains over the large schoolroom door honoring the lady in whose name the original donation for the school was made.

***

Side view of Kiambogo building

Rift Valley Academy, although a small school, still aspired to give its students a quality education and a solid preparation for children who would be going on to colleges and universities in the United States and elsewhere in the world. Lee Downing was asked to teach Latin, algebra, and Bible. One of his former students, Bernice Dalziel, recalls him not only as an excellent teacher who prepared her all the way up to Senior Cambridge School Certificate entrance exams in Latin, but as one who showed unusual understanding of children on the occasion when she broke a string of pearls. Although they were only inexpensive imitation pearls, Lee realized how much they meant to this child. He got down on his hands and knees with the students and searched under desks and tables until most of the beads were retrieved. At least there were enough to restring. That incident gave him a lasting place in that little girl's heart.

Lee was also gifted musically, and Bernice recalls his starting a choir for African males that the RVA students enjoyed hearing. Dr. William Barnett, another former student, recalls enjoying the Sunday afternoons when it was Downing's turn to take the afternoon services at RVA. In those days the church service in English was held in the afternoon in the largest schoolroom in the Kiambogo building at RVA. The missionary men took turns with the preaching. All too often the sermons were geared to the adults, while the children endured seemingly endless preaching that was well above their ability to understand. These afternoons became an endurance contest until someone like Lee Downing tried to remember the youngsters in his audience and brought his lessons down to their level of understanding.

Lucile Andersen (now Highstreet) remembers that Mr. Downing was not only an excellent Latin teacher but that he also had a phenomenal knowledge of Scripture. He memorized lengthy portions, and she believes he knew the whole book of Philippians by heart. It amazed her to find a man who was able to bring up chapter and verse so easily and then be able to quote so much without the help of a text. He also had a wonderful way of making the Bible real and understandable at the level of the students.

She also recalls that when her mother, Vivian Andersen, moved to Kijabe from Litein with her three little girls after the death of her husband, Andrew, they were housed in the old office building next door to the Downings. One day as Lee walked by he noticed that the little girls were up in the fig trees without sweaters. He thought they must be cold and suggested to Mrs. Andersen that the girls should wear sweaters. Lee seemed very concerned with the well-being of the girls and often stopped by on the way to Sunday services to walk with them. Margaret Andersen (now Schilling) was worried that Lee was more than interested in their well-being and worried that Lee and her mother might get together. She was determined that nobody should take the place of her daddy!

Olive Downey, another RVAite, related a story about Lee Downing and his love for teaching Latin. Lee felt it was important to pronounce Latin correctly, even though it was not a spoken language. His comment was that we do not pronounce *beau-ti-ful* broken up into syllables, but rather as a single word, *beautiful*. So Latin also deserved correct pronunciation, and Lee saw that his students did the right thing for this honored ancient language.

Olive Downey also told of an instance in the 1920s or '30s when some unexpected money was placed into her father's mission account. Accepting this as a special gift provided by God, William Downey, being a very generous person, quickly shared the windfall, putting it to good use. Before long the error was discovered. The money was mistakenly placed into the Down*ey* account rather than the Down*ing* account. Although Olive did not know how the money problem was ultimately resolved, its result was that the William Downeys and the Lee Downings became good friends.

Marie and Emil Sywulka, parents of Edward, a student at RVA who was later one of the famous Westervelt Boys, recounted a visit to the Kijabe church shortly after the murder of Hulda J. Stumpf in January 1930. Miss Stumpf was a close neighbor to the Downings, making the tragedy very personal. After the murder, church attendance among the Africans went way down, and Lee suffered both from the tragedy and also from the discouragement regarding those who had claimed Christianity and now failed to even attend church. Marie reported that, although he had become quite feeble, he continued pushing himself to be active and maintained his teaching of Latin at RVA.

His daughter Lucile recalled her father as the Latin and algebra teacher. With only one or two others in her classes, her turn to recite came up often, which was both good and bad. There was no time to relax while others were in the spotlight. This was probably good for the Latin learning, but hard on student nerves.

Several times in those early years the school was closed for a short period due to lack of personnel. The Downing kids were expected to keep up with their studies despite the closing of school. Now Lucile found herself in the position of having to respond to every question posed by her father. His piercing blue eyes seemed to bore into her very soul as she sought to respond to his questions. During these school closures Blanche tutored Lucile in history, using the meager library available to instill in her daughter a love for historical novels. Although Lucile felt she benefited from the special tutoring during these school closures, she was always glad to get back into class with other students who could share the scrutiny.

***

The early years of struggle in establishing the Rift Valley Academy saw it flourish under some wonderfully dedicated people, such as Theodore and Josephine Hope Westervelt, Muriel Perrott, Mary Slater, the William Blaikies, Le Roy and Emma Farnsworth, Fred and Betty McKenrick, and many others who, though perhaps not as dedicated or gifted, played a part in the building of the school. The Westervelts, who were one of the earliest families to devote their time to RVA, found that Josephine's health could not handle Kijabe's "harsh" environment. They found it harsh because it is cold and windy, and during the rainy season, wet. They returned to the United States and eventually opened their home to a dozen or more big, strapping RVA boys who needed a place to live while attending school in the United States after leaving RVA. The Westervelt Home grew into a large institution that became home to hundreds of missionaries' children over the years.

In 1930, the McKenricks worked at Githumu for about three years before moving to Kijabe to work at Moffatt Bible School while the Charles Teasdales were on furlough. When the Teasdales returned, the McKenricks moved to RVA as *homemakers*, the term used at RVA for many years for the people who made a home away from home for the students. They stayed until 1935.

The McKenrick's daughter, Flora, commonly known as Florene McKenrick (now Eddings), recalls when Herbert and Mildred Downing arrived to teach at RVA. Mildred was her French teacher, and although Mildred was a good teacher, Florene hated French. She remembers Herbert as the orchestra leader. There weren't many students at RVA, maybe only thirty, but she especially recalls Phillip Davis, the son of Dr. Elwood and Bernice Davis and, although he only attended one year, Bob Horn, a gold miner's son from Kakamega. At age eighteen, Florene went to the Westervelt Home to continue her education.

Despite the early struggles, RVA continued to grow and to maintain a high standard of education for the students. By the 1930s, it was accepting children of people who were not missionaries but who wanted a quality education or found the location convenient. The school embraced these children as another way of spreading the Gospel and influencing their ex-pat community.

7.

Herbert Caldwell Downing

Herbert Caldwell Downing was born at Kijabe on August 14, 1905, just before the Downings' first furlough. The middle name Caldwell was chosen by Lee, who remembered with fondness the couple who finally gave him a more permanent home when he and his brother

Herbert Caldwell Downing

were in the foster care system. Having been only ten when orphaned, he embraced the Caldwells, who accepted him into their hearts and home.

So, having a girl and a boy brought great happiness to the Downings. It also elevated their status with the local Africans. Sons were prized in the culture, as "real" men should produce sons. Of course there was no understanding of the male's contributing his X or his Y chromosome to determine the sex of the child. Hence many women found themselves tossed aside or had to accept their husband's taking a second or even a third wife because they only produced girls.

When the family returned to Kenya from their first furlough, Herbert, now three years old, began picking up both English and Kikuyu quickly and easily. It was not long before he was jabbering in Kikuyu as well as English. It was obvious early on that he had inherited his father's gift for languages as he easily shifted between the two languages. He also exhibited a good singing voice as well as a bent toward music. Fortunately, among the mission family at Kijabe, there were those who could develop both of these talents.

Now they were living in their nice, big, brick two-story home with its circular driveway leading to the front porch entrance framed in Blanche's legendary roses. It seemed that there were always guests requiring additional attention and especially good manners. Lucile and Herbert found that they were expected to speak and act appropriately at all times, but especially when company was present. Blanche managed to find little jobs that small children could do, instilling in her children a work ethic that never failed them.

Just months after their return to Kijabe from their first furlough, Kenneth Lee was born on June 26, 1908. With the family expanding and the house often filled with guests, the vegetable garden outdoors and the piano and organ indoors were often put to good use.

Even though Lucile and Herbert were given chores, they found time for plenty of play. The Downing children did not have lots of store-bought toys, but were able to improvise and create their own. Spools left after the thread was used up could make wonderful little tractors with the use of rubber bands and a stick. A piece of paper cut the right way made a great pinwheel that could catch the wind and whirl around just like a windmill. With a little imagination and ingenuity almost any rock could be transformed into some special animal or object. Perhaps it was those types of activities that developed in the Downing boys their many and varied gifts. As they grew up they were adept at building, mechanics, and maintenance jobs of different and sundry types.

It was believed by the early missionaries that the high altitude at Kijabe made it unwise for children to exert themselves riding a bicycle. Some of the missionary men rode bicycles, but the Downing children were not among the children who had bicycles because it was deemed too strenuous for the heart. Getting to most places on the station required walking down hill; then there was always the uphill climb back. It was also believed that the altitude and proximity to the equator made it necessary to wear double felt hats during daytime hours. If the house had a *mabati* roof one wore one's hat, even in the house, because it was believed that the sun's rays could penetrate through the metal.

Although we do not know how old Herbert was when the following incident happened, it gives a little insight as to his inquiring mind. Herbert, being handy with tools, and wanting to have a bicycle, decided he would just make one. He was able to find two wheels someplace and managed to attach a board across them to form his bicycle. The trouble came when he tried to ride his invention—the wheels would not turn! Although he was disappointed, this experience went into his knowledge of why and how the wheel works.

Lucile, Herbert and Kenneth

***

When she became of school age, Lucile joined the little group taught by Josephine Hope (later Westervelt) in the small mud-and-wattle hut with a dirt floor, *americani* ceiling, and canvas covering the rough walls. At this time, the number of children in the school was increasing, and it soon became evident that a larger school building was necessary. Josephine and Charles Hurlburt drew plans for a school that would accommodate forty students, which they were sure would forever be more than adequate to meet the anticipated number of children.

Rift Valley Academy's Kiambogo building was erected and remains today overlooking the beautiful Kedong Valley high on the east wall of the Great Rift Valley. How surprised Josephine and Charles would be to visit Kijabe today and find nearly five hundred students and multiple buildings scattered over a large campus. Kiambogo, which contains the root word *mbogo* (Swahili for buffalo), was named for the herds of Cape buffalo that used to roam the area. The powerful beast was chosen as the school's mascot and symbol.

Because the Downings lived on the station, their children were day students and lived at home. Lucile recalled one school term when her mother became ill and Lee took Blanche to the coast to recuperate. Kenneth was not in school yet so accompanied his parents to Mombasa while Lucile and Herbert became boarding students. Lucile found it difficult being away from her parents; it is not known how Herbert adjusted. This brief experience did give them insight into the emotion of homesickness and separation from parents that is so much a part of the experience of missionary children.

In 1913, the Downings again went on furlough. Lucile and Herbert were placed in a public school in the United States. During this furlough Lee made a trip to England to discuss mission matters and the relationship of the British missionary and American missionary under the Africa Inland Mission.

After their furlough the Lee Downings returned to Kenya and to Kijabe. By now all three children were school age and once again attended RVA as day students. Lucile, the eldest, was high school age. It became apparent that the family would need to consider her future, as opportunities for college were not available in Kenya. In 1920, when she had completed her high school studies with special tutoring at RVA, the family once again headed for the United States. Herbert had completed the ninth grade, and Kenneth was in sixth grade.

With the children settled into schools in the United States and approaching adulthood, Lee and Blanche returned to Kenya in 1925.

After completing high school at Muskingum Academy, Herbert followed the family tradition and enrolled at Muskingum College, New Concord, Ohio where his major was liberal arts. Paying for his college required working as a lab technician in a dental office. As usual this young man absorbed what was going on at his work and learned a great deal about dentistry. After five years he was able to complete requirements for his bachelor of arts degree. Wanting specific knowledge in areas not provided at Muskingum, Herbert took several classes at Ohio State University.

It was at Muskingum that he noticed a beautiful young lady with a peaches-and-cream complexion and curly red hair. The more he found out about her the more intrigued he became. He was delighted when Mildred Houk accepted his proposal to become his wife.

Mildred Susanna Houk

Mildred Susanna Houk was born in Pennsylvania on December 13, 1907. Her father was a Presbyterian minister in Freeport,

Mildred Susanna Houk

Pennsylvania, so she grew up in a manse with all the plus-and-minus attributes of that type of upbringing. At age seven she committed her life to Christ and began seeking God's will for her life. After completing high school in Clayton, Pennsylvania, she enrolled at Muskingum College. After two years of college her father suggested she get a temporary teaching certificate, which she did by attending Washington and Jefferson College summer school in Washington, Pennsylvania. He then arranged a teaching position for her in Ellwood City, Pennsylvania.

Because her father was a preacher and these were Depression years, times were tough. By taking classes during the summer, she finally got her degree and teaching certificate from Muskingum in 1929. Herbert, who had graduated in 1928, had been teaching in New Concord High School. Mildred taught summer school at Muskingum College in order to pay off her college loans.

Mildred's brother, Dale, who was the supervising principal at the California High School, in California, Pennsylvania, recognized in Herbert a real giftedness in many areas, especially industrial arts. He persuaded Herbert to go with him to California, Pennsylvania, to install a school shop. When Dale transferred to Forest Hills, Pennsylvania, he again wanted Herbert to get a shop going for that school, and also to be junior high principal.

During this whole time Herbert and Mildred had been attracted to each other. Mildred soon learned that Herbert was committed to missions and felt that God would use his ability with the Kikuyu language to minister to those people. If she were to marry him, she would have to be committed to missionary service in Africa. Feeling that this was what God had in mind for her, she willingly accepted both Herbert's proposal for marriage and the commitment to mission service. Even before they were married they applied to Africa Inland Mission.

With their sights set on Africa, they were married June 19, 1931. Mildred taught in the public elementary school and in Bloomfield High School. During the summer, she taught algebra and trigonometry at Muskingum. Most of her students were other teachers already employed in local schools and seeking to upgrade their skills or

Herbert and Mildred's wedding, June 19, 1931
Kenneth, Blanche, Herbert, Mildred, her parents, Mildred
and Clarence Houk, her sister, Margaret, and a niece, Billy Jean Houk

working on teaching certificates. All the while, Mildred was gaining valuable teaching experience she would use in the future.

The young couple immediately began to work toward leaving for Kenya. They had joined Africa Inland Mission with the full intention of working with the Africans, probably in one of the established stations, and probably in the educational endeavors of the group.

Knowing that Herbert and Mildred had already applied to AIM and were hoping to get to Africa sometime, Herbert's father, who was in the United States on furlough, called to say they could get passage for Africa on March 10, 1933.

During this waiting period Mildred had learned that she was expecting their first child. Gayle Margaret was born May 15, 1932. While they were delighted, it did add complications to travel and support issues. Having grown up in Kenya, Herbert did not worry as much as Mildred did about taking a ten-month-old baby out to "darkest Africa."

While Herbert resigned his position as principal and dispersed or sold their worldly goods, Mildred went with Gayle to her family in New Concord, Ohio. With mixed feelings of fear for the unknown, anticipation for the adventure, and sadness as she anticipated five long years before being with her family again, Mildred bravely fit into the plans being laid out for her.

In August 1931 Lee and Blanche had taken another furlough. When they returned to Kenya this time, they would have two of their children with them, now in the capacity of missionaries.

***

At midnight on March 10, 1933, the S.S. *Hamburg* sailed, carrying Lee and Blanche, Herbert, Mildred and Gayle, and Kenneth. With them were more AIMers: Charles and Mae Teasdale with son Ted, Dr. and Mrs. Ralph Kleinschmidt with daughters Edith and Esther, and Augusta Dakin.

One of their first experiences with the faith issue to which AIM adhered concerned their passports. President Roosevelt had closed the banks because of the Depression, making it impossible for them to cash checks to pay for the passports. Fortunately the money for the four Downing passports was given by a friend, Edith McIntyre. Mr. Teasdale had also been given a cash offering, so he acted as banker for the group during the trip. Little did they anticipate what the future held for them as they sailed for Kenya that dark night in 1933.

The trip was not uneventful. The little baby of one of the young German families on board died and had to be buried at sea. Father

Downing was invited to be with the sorrowing family. Realizing that Mildred's parents might be anxious about her, Lee cabled what he thought was a reassuring message. "Mother and Mildred mildly sick." Unfortunately the message arrived with this wording: "Mother and Mildred mildly sink."

After reaching Southampton, where they would wait for ongoing passage on the S.S. *Nyassa*, Herbert and Mildred took the opportunity to take the train to London to meet with the British Home Council of AIM. Blanche took care of Gayle so that Herbert and Mildred could make this trip more easily. Not having done much traveling in the past, Mildred thoroughly enjoyed seeing London and the English countryside.

Unfortunately, Mac Teasdale had to remain in London as she had become quite ill, so Charles and Ted remained with her, but they were all able to rejoin the ship in Genoa.

Experiencing being in a place where English was not always understood, Mildred got a taste of what was coming in Kenya. At a stop in Lisbon, without knowing Portuguese, Mildred successfully used her limited Spanish to get a thermos of hot water for Gayle's Similac. But in Kenya, where she knew nothing comparable to Kikuyu, she was going to have to learn it from the beginning.

Going through the Bay of Biscay, Blanche once again became very seasick and Mildred joined her discomfort, making it necessary for Herbert to take over the care of Gayle. He found himself washing and hanging diapers, rocking the baby in her new pram that the grandparents bought for her in Southampton, and feeding her Similac.

Their journey took them past Gibraltar, through the Mediterranean Sea, and on through the Suez Canal. On April 16, 1933, the ship finally docked at Mombasa, and their African adventures began.

8.

Herbert and Mildred: Rift Valley Academy, 1933–1937

Their ship arrived in Mombasa late in the day, just as the upcountry train heading for Nairobi was due to leave the station. Using his considerable powers of persuasion, Charles Teasdale talked the train personnel into putting the party of fourteen aboard. Herbert, Mildred and Gayle had a private compartment. Although their accommodations were comfortable, sleep was hard to come by. The train stopped every twenty minutes at one small station after another along its route. Here hawkers appeared at the windows attempting to sell passengers whatever wares they could or simply to beg.

For Mildred this was all very exciting and new. Since the train did not get into Nairobi until about eight the next morning, she was able to see the beautiful scenery and even some of the animals as the train slowly made its way deeper into the heart of Kenya. For Herbert and Kenneth it was coming home. They immediately enjoyed speaking Kikuyu and found they had lost very little in the years away. The day was spent in town, and that evening they stayed at Mayfield, the mission guesthouse in Nairobi.

In the morning, wearing their double felt hats acquired in Alexandria, Egypt, they were ready to face the tropical sun and the high altitude of Kijabe. The local people had been made aware of the Downings' return and were out in force to welcome them back. Here were Herbert and Kenneth all grown up, and Herbert with

The Downing family appropriately dressed for the equatorial sun. Herbert, Gayle, Mildred, Kenneth, Blanche, Lee H, 1933

a wife and baby! The Downings' cook, Gicoya, whom Blanche had trained, prepared a good dinner. Mildred was immediately impressed by being served a good green salad, something they had not had on the long voyage.

Their first month was spent with the elder Downings in the big brick house. Mildred heard the stories of the leopard exploring the house at night, the murder of Hulda Stumpf in her house that was close by, and other tales. There was no electricity, no telephone, and no indoor sanitation. Needless to say she was a bit uneasy when left alone in the house one night. She survived that night, and many others through the years, by learning to rely on the promise "the Lord is our keeper."

With three Downing men now at Kijabe, people began calling Lee "Father Downing" to help keep them straight. Father Downing wrote up the following incident that happened soon after their arrival in 1933, near the time Ken left to work at Githumu. It is shown here exactly as Lee typed it out.

Shooting a Buffalo

For many weeks an old, lone buffalo bull, banished from the herd by his fellows, had been making periodic visits to the native gardens on the most distant part of our mission estate. It came only at night, and usually three or four nights in succession then was absent for perhaps a week. It had almost devastated one garden near the border in which was big corn almost ripe. The owner begged Herbert to come up at night and try to shoot it. He even constructed a platform in a tree in the garden where he would be safe and could make himself comfortable with blankets.

Herbert and Kenneth spent several hours one night in the tree with rifles and spotlight from a car. They heard it feeding at a distance, and when it was doubtful whether it would come nearer, they turned the light on, and it immediately bolted. Some time later, the owner informed them that it was again frequenting the gardens so they spent an entire night in the tree, but it did not return.

After Kenneth went to Githumu Herbert learned that it was again making nightly visits and consented to try once more. He and the owner of the garden had just taken their places on the platform

Cape Buffalo
Photo courtesy Don Moris

about 7:30 P.M. when they heard it in the adjoining garden. They waited in hope of its coming nearer. An hour passed and it seemed to be moving farther away. Herbert told the native to turn on the light and they could just see it leaving the garden. He shot but missed it; he fired again and the ball struck it in the hip, but did not bring it down. They decided not to follow it in the dark, but to spend the night in a native hut nearby. Soon after daybreak they started on its track. In a little while they came to an area of dense bush in the forest, and near to the kraal of the chief of the Andorobo, who is an experienced big game hunter.

He and his son, also an experienced hunter, joined them, taking with them two trained dogs. Herbert said it was most interesting to watch those dogs work. One went ahead of the men and the other behind them very quietly with their heads uplifted and continually sniffing. They would go back and forth, a little to the right then a little to the left of the path broken through the bush by the buffalo. Herbert said he would have been afraid to enter that jungle without those keen scented dogs accompanying them. Presently they reached an area of bush isolated from the rest. All walked around this and could find no tracks leading beyond, so they concluded it must be within that area.

During the night Herbert had been committing the whole matter definitely to the Lord, and this text was brought repeatedly to his mind: "Commit thy way unto the Lord; trust also in him; and he shall bring it to pass." (Ps. 37:5).

With this promise in mind he was able to tell all the others to remain at the point where the buffalo entered the bush until he could go alone around to the opposite side, then for them to follow along the path, and he would be ready to shoot, if it should come out near him. In a little while he heard the dogs bark and then a sound as of the animal coming slowly toward him. Presently he saw its back above the bushes and a moment later it emerged with its head close to the ground. He aimed at its neck and the shot brought it to the ground with a terrible groan. It lay there tossing its head vigorously but could not rise. He waited a few minutes then walked closer and gave it a finishing shot in the forehead.

It was an old animal and very large. The distance between the tips of its horns was 35 1/2 inches. In the interval between two of Herbert's visits the natives had dug a pit 8 feet deep in the path by which it usually came and covered it over. Into this it fell, but was able to horn sufficient dirt from the side and trample it under foot to get out.

There was great rejoicing over the death of this buffalo, as it was not only destroying the people's food, but they were in constant fear of being attacked on the paths. The Andorobo told the native foreman of our agricultural department that if "Bwana Herberti" would drink "njohi" (the intoxicating beer they make) they would give him all he wanted.

Herbert brought the skin, head (with horns in place), feet and rounds of meat to his house, and let the natives have the rest. Nothing remains, not even what we call "refuse," when they have access to a slaughtered animal.

The rifle he used was a Mauser, 9.3 millimeter, or .366". It was shot within 300 yards of the place where Mr. Devitt shot the elephant last June.

Lee H. Downing

Although they had anticipated working in the African schools, after meeting with the Field Council, Herbert and Mildred were asked to take over the Rift Valley Academy. The Field Council was the governing body that oversaw the missionaries and the general work of the mission. Their educational background and Herb's ability as a school administrator were considered to make them a natural fit for that position. They agreed to this work, and their assignment was never changed. The school at that time was only about thirty students, accommodating a mix of missionary children and the children of settlers who were in Kenya as farmers, miners, hunters, and a myriad of other occupations. Most of the non-mission children were British, making it necessary to incorporate some subjects they would need. Consequently British history and math using British money became part of the curriculum.

Quickly Herbert adjusted to being the jack-of-all-trades so necessary for the missionary. He was the chief administrator, teacher of math, band and orchestra leader, and constantly the liaison between the local Africans, the mission, and the school. His fluency with Kikuyu was invaluable.

Mildred also stepped into teaching Latin, French, and some math courses. Whatever subject was needed for the students the Downings either taught themselves or found someone to cover the classes. Subtly and quietly the school began to gain in stature and reputation.

The Principal's House
William Blaikie's; Herb Downing's; Ken Downing's

Herbert and Mildred moved into the house formerly occupied by the William Blaikies. It was a dark, rat-infested place with little to recommend it. Although they still repulsed her, Mildred soon learned how to deal with mice, lizards, and other creatures that wanted to share their dwelling. She had to learn to cook on a wood stove in a kitchen that was in a separate building from the main house. She had a difficult time communicating with the African help and getting them to do what she wanted.

Purchasing supplies required shopping at little Indian *dukas* three miles away down at the railway station. To get there was a chore over bumpy, rutted roads on a mule, by foot, or in the

Mildred rides a mule for shopping

ox-cart. Washing had to be done on a washboard and hung on a clothesline. This could be a problem during the rainy season when clothes had to be hung on racks around the house and rotated in front of the fireplace in order to get them dry. Ironing was done using flat irons heated on the wood stove. It seemed that all household chores were indeed that, chores that took so much more time than the same tasks had taken at home in the United States. Having African help was nice after they were trained and when one could communicate with them. Still, there were days when it seemed it would just be easier to do it oneself rather than have to retell, demonstrate again and again, and then, too often, redo.

The Herbert Downings had not been in Kenya long when Blanche died on November 4, 1933, of liver cancer. She was buried in the cemetery at Kijabe. Lee felt his ministry as field director was over. However, as a man of prayer his influence continued. Mildred established a daily prayer meeting for all able to attend each afternoon at four o'clock. She remembered many times that Lee would share a specific answer to his prayer. When a problem arose he would firmly state, "Let's just pray about it."

**

Herbert and Mildred's first son, Glenn Herbert, arrived at Kijabe Hospital on January 22, 1935. For this experience Mildred walked up the hill to the hospital accompanied by Herbert and Blanche Kala, an African helper. Mildred had two missionary nurses attending but no doctor. The nurses were Bessie Stevenson and Ida Rhodes. An African helper named Salome who worked at the hospital also assisted. In the morning, Father Downing placed the general call signaling an important event to all houses at Kijabe mission. This was done by grinding a very long ring on the inter-station party-line telephone. Since the annual conference was in session, attended by missionaries from all the smaller stations, Glenn received a big welcome.

Now, with school lessons, caring for Gayle and Glenn, attending or hosting the daily prayer meetings, entertaining guests, and restructuring the old dark house, Mildred found her hands too full. Herbert was trying to make the house more habitable by putting glass in the doors and making a window over the stair landing. Since there was no electricity, they had to use oil lamps that burned kerosene. These necessitated cleaning glass globes and trimming wicks. Even with clean globes and trimmed wicks, they did not give a really good light.

**

At the time the Downings were assigned to RVA, there were only two students living on Kijabe station, Gayle Downing and Ted Teasdale. In 1934, Lucile Andersen was added to the station kids when her family moved to Kijabe. The rest were boarding students, with Mr. and Mrs. Fred McKenrick as homemakers. For all these children ranging from first to eighth grades there were three teachers: Ruth Truesdell, who was the headmistress, Edith Holman (later Devitt) who was studying Kikuyu with the plan to get into African work, and Erica Lany, one of the older students pressed into service. Herbert and Mildred picked up the slack. Fortunately, Lee Downing enjoyed teaching Latin and Bible and agreed to continue.

Fred McKenrick was involved with African church work, teaching Kikuyu language classes to missionaries, and supervising the RVA dormitory. His heavy workload finally resulted in a nervous breakdown, and he was sent upcountry where he could be under a doctor's care. The Field Council asked Herbert and Mildred to take over the role of dormitory supervision, along with their classes, children, and other obligations, until the Paul Lehrers arrived. Mildred's comment: "All I can say about this period is: We survived."

Paul and Elizabeth Lehrer finally arrived, and that put Herbert and Mildred back into their original heavy load. In comparison to when they had been so overburdened, their responsibilities now did not seem quite as heavy.

***

Perhaps some comments on early staffing for RVA are appropriate. In the early life of AIM and RVA, teaching missionaries' children was not considered mission work, especially by supporters in the United States. Consequently, in order to staff the school, many newcomers were placed as teachers while in language study. Those who learned language easily did not have to remain at RVA long. Those less able stayed longer. The Herbert Downings were victims of this unfortunate misunderstanding of mission work, for, as soon as they were assigned to RVA, one of their main contributors dropped their support because they were not doing "mission" work. This left the Downings on the field without adequate finances and no place to get more. In God's marvelous way, He supplied their daily needs but there was nothing left over.

In 1937 it came time for their first furlough. They had no money for passage, but Father Downing assured them that he was sure the Lord wanted them to go. Mildred was expecting her third baby, so if they were to go, it needed to be soon. Mildred thought, *Impossible.* A few days later Herbert got a letter from a shipping company in Mombasa telling them that the company had been instructed to provide passage. The Downings were to pick up their tickets from the purser. Herbert had never heard of anything like this, so he sent a telegram to verify the accuracy of this message. The response came back immediately that indeed it was accurate and the Downings were to hurry on down to the coast. Packing quickly, Herbert, Mildred, Gayle, and Glenn headed for Mombasa. Myrtle Zaffke, a mission nurse, was also traveling on the ship, which gave Mildred some comfort. They sailed on the S.S. *West Isleta* going around South Africa for New York.

Daughter Gayle recalls a learning experience from that trip. The Downing family found they were part of a group of twelve passengers on the freighter. As with most little children, Gayle began to get a little bored with the look of open waters and no land in sight, so she eagerly anticipated the first port of call, Port Elizabeth in South Africa. When the day arrived she was mortified when her mother selected her least favorite dress to wear ashore. It was a white organdy with blue narrow stripes that formed geometric patterns that crisscrossed each other. It had a white, square collar and a high yoke from which the gathered skirt fell, but it had no waistline. Gayle hated that dress with a passion. After she protested, causing a minor scene, Herbert said these fateful words: "She is not going ashore." There was no arguing. No second chances. Gayle did not go ashore.

But when her parents returned to the ship, they did bring her first-ever "paper hankies," and many of the other passengers and sailors brought her goodies. However, the lesson was learned: one does not argue and throw even minor tantrums; one does as one is told.

A friend, Edith McIntyre, along with Mildred's brothers, Ed and Glenn Houk, met the ship when it arrived in New York on November 3, 1937. Seeing Mildred so "great with child," Edith offered to pay for their way home by train—by Pullman, no less! (Having had an apparent change of heart, this was the lady who had dropped her support because Herbert and Mildred were not working with Africans.) Mildred's brothers took the luggage by car to the Houk home in New Concord, Ohio.

Fred Lanning, who was AIM business manager at the time, asked Herbert who had authorized their passage, because he had not. Herbert did not have an answer but recognized God's provision for them at the right moment. Eventually Herbert and Mildred were able to pay for the tickets that had appeared from nowhere!

The world was in troubled times; World War II started in 1939, and for the duration, passage by ship was denied people with children.

Herbert and Mildred would not be able to return to Kenya until 1947. In the meantime RVA would find itself under the leadership of another Downing.

9.

Kenneth Lee Downing

Kenneth Lee Downing

Kenneth, third child and second son of Lee and Blanche, had been born June 26, 1908, at Kijabe. Herbert was two and a half years old and Lucile five and a half. With her three young children and constant visitors who usually stayed for several days to weeks, Blanche had her hands full. Fortunately, she was a good manager and had some well-trained African help who lessened the cooking and cleaning chores. Lee was serving as field director so found it necessary to be away from home much too often to suit Blanche. With road conditions and transportation problems, his trips often took him distances from Kijabe that meant days on the road and away from home.

Lucile was old enough to find her new baby brother a fun baby doll. She enjoyed playing with him but was happy to give him back to Blanche. Most of the missionaries had trained an African girl to help with the children, so it is probably correct that Blanche had someone to watch Herbert and Kenneth when she was busy with some of her other duties.

When Lucile was old enough, she joined the small group of students being taught by Josephine Hope. Three years later Herbert joined his sister at school. By this time classes had moved into the rooms adjacent to the Kijabe Chapel, and eventually they moved into Kiambogo.

When the Downings left for furlough in October 1920, they remained in the United States for five years. By then the children were young adults. Lucile and Herbert were already enrolled at Muskingum College, and it was time for Kenneth to follow family tradition. He had one more year of high school, which he took at Smithfield (Ohio)

High School before enrolling at Muskingum College, graduating with his BA in math and physics.

The Lee Downings returned to Kenya in November 1925 to resume their work, leaving the three children at home to pursue their higher education. Lucile had become a high school teacher and an organist for her church. On January 19, 1928, at age twenty-five, she married Robert Sawhill in Pennsylvania. She did not get back to Kenya until many years later when she returned to visit in 1964. The Lee Downings took their next furlough in 1931 and returned in March of 1933, accompanied by both their sons. Herb was now married to Mildred, and little Gayle was not quite two.

Both Herbert and Kenneth returned to Kenya with the intention of going into African work, but God and the AIM had other needs and would soon tap Herbert and Mildred for working at RVA.

***

Herbert and Kenneth experience snow in the USA

Ken was a larger man than his brother, standing a few inches taller and structurally more solid and robust-looking. He took after his mother in stature and had developed into a man who gave the appearance of one who was in authority and one with whom to be reckoned. Herbert had taken after his father with his slight build.

During the years just preceding the arrival of Herbert and Kenneth, Africa Inland Mission had struggled with the problem of education for the Africans. Some felt that mission work should focus on evangelism and that it was not in the parameters of mission work to be teaching reading and writing to the African children. Others felt that schools were an excellent way to accomplish the task of evangelism by getting the children when young and preparing them to read the Scriptures and ultimately to take on leadership in their own country. Finally, the group feeling that education was a good method of doing mission work prevailed.

Ken stepped into this climate on his arrival. This decision meant that AIM now had to deal with the government, which would be providing most of the money and therefore would have some say regarding the operation of the schools. The British colonial government was generally happy to have the missions take on this responsibility and gave them free reign as to curriculum and methods.

With Ken's educational background and his fluency with Kikuyu, as well as his knowledge of the local people and customs, he was the natural selection to get the work of local schools underway. Githumu was considered the best location for this, as he would need to be in a position to travel to locations throughout Kikuyu-land where schools would be built and require supervision.

Githumu is about sixty miles from Kijabe. With weather permitting and good roads, it is relatively close. But with rain and mud, the trip between the two places can take the better part of a day. Schools began to crop up all over the district, making it more convenient for the little children to walk to school. Each new school required teachers, materials, and buildings. Finding trained Kenyan teachers was a major problem, requiring the hiring of many teachers with an education probably equivalent to elementary school. Some missionaries were recruited to teach in the schools, giving some help in the area of standards. As time went on and the local people were able to gain higher skills, this problem began to disappear to some extent.

The job required Ken to travel to the surrounding communities making sure that the teachers were doing their work, making sure they were paid, and generally overseeing the operations of these "out-schools." This was a huge responsibility but one that suited Ken well.

***

Before the year of 1933 was over, Blanche became very ill and died on November 4. They had only been back in Kenya seven months. The doctors determined she died of liver cancer that went undetected until too late.

Following is a letter written to friends and family by Lee Downing regarding the death of Blanche, presented exactly as he wrote it.

Kijabe, Kenya Colony
East Africa
November 8, 1933

Dear Friends:

In reporting Mrs. Downing's last illness and departure to be with the Lord, I have in mind fellow-missionaries on the field and friends in the homeland. It is difficult to decide how much detail to give. I want you to have sufficient to appreciate how wonderfully the Lord has wrought for us.

On October 5th Dr. Shaw of the Scotch mission came to Kijabe (our doctor is on furlough) for tonsil operations on two of the RVA children, and we had him examine Mrs. Downing, as she had been suffering for several days from a pain in her right side. He found the liver greatly enlarged and recommended an examination by a specialist in Nairobi.

By wire I made an appointment with Dr. Burkitt for three o'clock the next day. We arrived on the 2:30 p.m. train and went directly to his office. He, with his assistant and nurse, examined her thoroughly. While doing so Mrs. Downing heard him say in a low tone to the nurse, "An enormous liver." Later he thought there was also an enormous abscess, probably the result of amoebic dysentery at some time. (The only time she had anything of the kind was in the Congo in 1931). He began daily injections of emetine. Soon he was not satisfied with the response and wanted her moved from our Mission Rest Home to the Maia Carberry Nursing Home next door for professional observation. This was done on October 17th. On the 21st she was X-rayed and the pictures revealed no organs diseased except the liver.

On the 24th she was operated on by Dr. Burkitt, assisted by Drs. McCaldin and Gregory, who are associated with him in practice. An incision was made into the pleural cavity in order to determine how far up the swollen liver extended and to place a packing of gauze boiled in

Vaseline to prevent pus reaching the lung in case the supposed abscess should burst into the pleural cavity. A needle was then inserted below the diaphragm through which they expected to draw any pus. When four attempts in different directions failed to disclose any abscess, they decided the enlargement must be due to some other cause, and probably cancer. A few days' further observation proved it beyond question. The liver was a cancerous mass, almost as hard as a stone, the doctor said, and how she had lived so long in such a condition and have so short a period of extreme suffering, he could not understand. As soon as it was known that her condition was beyond natural remedies, strong opiates were used which relieved almost entirely the suffering. Her mind was clear to the last, and she talked freely about heaven and the loved ones to be left behind.

Kenneth and I were with her daily from the time of her operation and Herbert a part of the time including the last day.

When I entered her room early Tuesday morning, she said, "I thought I would be in heaven this morning, and I knew you would be glad." Later as Kenneth and I stood on opposite sides of the bed, each holding a hand, she looked at us and said, "Almost like heaven. How nice it would be if you could go too." We recorded her saying when speaking so that we have her exact words. Those on Wednesday included the following: "I'm so tired. It can't be long." "Do you think I will go home today? I hope so." "Forever at rest—forever and forever." "Precious Jesus, release me."

She was unable to speak on Friday and slept most of the time. A little after midnight (12:30 a.m. Saturday, November 4th) she peacefully passed into the Lord's presence, where for days she had longed to be.

Lee went on to describe in detail how he had bought a cedar coffin and how he and his sons had transported it to Kijabe. He told the details of the service and how Fred McKenrick and Charles Teasdale had officiated. The RVA children brought bouquets of flowers. He ended the letter assuring those in the homeland that the Maia Carberry Nursing Home was a well-equipped hospital, the doctors were excellent, and that Blanche had had the best possible care. (In fact, one of the doctors, Dr. Denis Burkitt, later gained worldwide recognition for his published research on a condition that came to be named Burkitt's Lymphoma.)

The many details Lee provided reflect much of the personality of this man. He was one who attended to details and cared about the small stuff, or to quote his daughter, he was a perfectionist.

Although Lucile was not with him, it was a great comfort to Lee having Herbert and Mildred and their family with him at Kijabe. Ken came into Nairobi from Githumu and stayed with him all during the last days when Blanche was in hospital. Lee returned to Kijabe and to the big brick house he had built for Blanche. Suddenly it seemed so big and so empty. Through the dark days, Lee spent many hours in his secret prayer garden and enjoyed his Father's comfort.

***

In October 1935, Ken returned to Kijabe where he moved in with his father to help him with his duties as field director. Ken continued with the supervision of schools around Githumu.

Feeling the need for a wife, Kenneth began to look over the prospects. There were quite a few young single ladies from whom to choose, although there were few single men. This made the competition among the ladies rather keen as they hoped to attract the attention of this eligible bachelor. After a time Kenneth decided that the lady he would pursue was Ruth Truesdell, who was teaching at RVA. The romance progressed to the delight of the couple and their many friends, and their engagement was announced at Christmas 1935.

But before Ken and Ruth were married, another single lady arrived at Kijabe. Ivy Ambrose, a nurse from Canada, was sent to Kijabe, where her assignment was to work in the "White Ward" of Theodora Hospital under Dr. Elwood Davis. After she arrived, she was reassigned to private nursing duty for an elderly missionary. In the meantime, Ken and Ruth were becoming more and more aware of incompatibility between them so broke off their engagement. No doubt, it was hard for Ruth to see a romance between Ken and Ivy quickly blossom.

The break-up caused tongues to wag and fellow workers to take sides. Some felt that Ivy had openly and brazenly pursued Ken, while others rationalized that his marriage to Ruth would doubtless have been a mistake. When talking over the matter with his father, Ken pointed out areas of difference that would probably have caused trouble between him and Ruth. Correspondence between Lee Downing, the then field director, and the Home Office suggests that things got rather testy. It was finally decided that Ken and Ivy should be asked to delay their marriage until after Ruth left for furlough, thus alleviating her hurt feelings, and perhaps stilling wagging tongues. This meant a wait of about three months, and then Ken and Ivy were married on March 2, 1937. Although Lee had thought Ruth to be a good match for Kenneth, he accepted his son's choice. In a warm letter written to Ivy during this waiting period, Lee assured her of his acceptance and of how he looked forward to calling her "daughter."

Time heals, and before long, Ivy made her way into the hearts of the community.

Ivy Winifred Ambrose Downing

Ivy was born on July 19, 1910, in Hamilton, Ontario, Canada. Her parents had emigrated from England. Hers was a Christian family, so she was attuned to listening for God's will and calling and decided that it was her calling to be a missionary nurse.

After graduating from the Canadian Bible Institute, she enrolled in the nursing program at Hamilton General Hospital in 1929, where

Ivy Ambrose Downing

she received her RN in 1932. While working as a graduate nurse, she applied to Africa Inland Mission and in late 1935 sailed on the S.S. *Deutschland* with a group of nine other missionaries, old and new, headed for Kenya, Tanganyika, and the Belgian Congo. They arrived in Mombasa January 2, 1936.

One of the advantages of these long voyages by ship was the opportunity of the new missionaries to arrive in Africa having a cadre of friendships already established.

Most of the ships carried several families and young singles. Some were returning to the field, and some were new missionaries needing reassurances and assistance with travel.

When notified that her goods had arrived in Nairobi, Ivy decided to leave them there until she had her final assignment, hoping to save the cost of a double shipment. As it turned out, she was assigned to Kijabe and would be working at the Theodora Hospital under the direction of Dr. Elwood Davis.

It was right about this time that Ken and Ruth mutually agreed to break off their engagement, and it wasn't long before romance sparked between Ken and Ivy. Many weeks of note and letter writing ensued, while the couple tried to be discreet and yet were unable to conceal their feelings. According to mission policy at the time, courting couples should not live on the same station. There was a real need for a nurse to fill in at the Githumu medical center, so Ivy was assigned to Githumu from October to December 1936. Finally on March 2, 1937, less than two years after Ivy's arrival on the field, Ken and Ivy were married.

The wedding took place at Kijabe with Herbert and Mildred as best man and matron of honor. After the wedding, a reception was held on the porch at RVA, with some of the older RVA girls serving the luncheon.

Kenneth and Ivy's wedding, March 2, 1937

Three weeks later, Lee wrote a description of the wedding to one of his cousins in Ohio, saying:

Kenneth and Ivy were married at 10 a.m. on March 2nd. All of our people seemed eager to contribute something to the happiness of the young couple. Mrs. Propst, Miss Rhodes, Mr. Lehrer and the R.V.A. children decorated the church, Mildred was matron of honor, and Herbert best man, Mr. Lehrer gave the bride away, I performed the ceremony and Mr. Teasdale led in prayer. The wedding march was played by Bernice Dalziel and five of

the other large school girls waited tables at the wedding luncheon—
served at R.V.A. under the direction of Mrs. Lehrer. Mr. and Mrs.
Lehrer and Ivy came out in the same party.

Ivy comes from Hamilton, Ontario, is a registered nurse and a
very practical young lady. She made her wedding dress, also the
dress which Mildred wore on the occasion. She plays the piano and
sings well. Is about two years younger than Kenneth and they seem
well adapted to each other. I am pleased with his choice and feel that
I have two lovely daughters-in-law. Both are just as considerate of
me as can be. To have Kenneth and Ivy with me in the home with me
is a great comfort. Her father is a contractor whose special trade is
brick-laying. Both parents are devoted Christians and are very nice
looking in their pictures. They write as people who know the Lord.

Soon after the luncheon they left by car for the two weeks'
honeymoon in the Lake District about 250 miles from here. On an
unoccupied station of the Friend's Mission is a furnished house
which was placed at their disposal where they expected to spend most
of their time, but after one week Mr. and Mrs. Ford (Jefferson and
Helen) of that mission invited them to accompany them on a business
trip to another mission station in Uganda 150 miles beyond. They
readily accepted and had a lovely journey over good roads and saw
much new country. They returned last Saturday evening and we are
comfortably settled together in this home.

And so Kenneth and Ivy were married, little realizing that their
lives would take strange twists and turns that they did not anticipate
were coming.

10.

Kenneth and Ivy: Rift Valley Academy, 1937–1947

With Herbert and Mildred leaving for furlough on September 1, 1937, RVA was once again left without a principal and with a smattering of teachers filtering through as they became available. Again the Field Council turned to the Downings. This time it was Kenneth who was asked to take over the school as acting principal. Ken was a trained teacher, and Ivy's training as a nurse was a good fit for the vacancy. Both would be doing teaching as needed and managing the school administration. They accepted the challenge and moved into the positions vacated by Herbert and Mildred.

Paul and Elizabeth Lehrer had arrived at Kijabe, having sailed

Paul and Elizabeth Lehrer
Photo courtesy Dr. Harold LaFont

on November 20, 1935, on the S.S. *Deutschland,* the same ship that brought Ivy Ambrose to Kenya. They had agreed to be house parents for the boarding students at RVA. Having had no children of their own, they appeared to be an ideal couple for taking over this assignment. Paul Lehrer would teach, maintain the dormitory duties, and do the bookwork connected with the boarding school. Elizabeth Lehrer would manage the housekeeping chores, supervise the kitchen and laundry, and generally manage the "home." By the time Herbert and Mildred left for furlough, the Lehrers were well established and into their roles, ready to carry on. With Ken and Ivy taking over the academic part of the school, things looked well under control.

The school was still relatively small, with thirty-five to forty students. Most of the children were boarders, with the majority from the homes of settlers and non-missionaries. Those attending had to accept the fact that their children would be nurtured in a Christian community and required to take Bible instruction daily. For many of these settlers' children and some of their families, the training at Kijabe resulted in their becoming Christians. For AIM this was another method of evangelization and also another reason for the existence of the school. The tuition paid by the non-AIM students helped with the expenses and made it possible to have classes of more than one student in each grade.

The relative newlyweds, Ken and Ivy, moved into what Mildred still called the Blaikie house but soon became known as the KLD house. With the renovations Herbert had done, it was not as gloomy or dark as it had been originally. The location was ideal, slightly off campus but still within very close walking distance of the main Kiambogo building.

In order to make room for Ken and Ivy, Herbert and Mildred stored a lot of their things in the attic of the house, anticipating they would be back within a year or two to resume their responsibilities at RVA. Ivy began to make this her home by decorating as much as was possible with what belongings the young couple had between them. They had no idea that their "interim" assignment would stretch into a decade.

The front of the house faced the Great Rift Valley and shared the same spectacular view as that enjoyed by the students living in the main Kiambogo building. However, the front entrance to the house was placed such that it was usually more convenient for visitors to enter at the back door that was off the walkway between the main house and kitchen building. Around the house was a hedge that became quite high as time went on, giving the house a secluded feeling and separating it from the school. A few well-placed plants broke up the otherwise austere exterior.

***

The school Ken and Ivy inherited had its own share of problems. Finding teachers was a constant source of concern, as coming to the mission field specifically to teach missionaries' children was still not understood as mission work. Therefore, one had to use people assigned there by the Field Council while doing language study or coerced into giving some time before they were able to escape into their first choice of assignment. Some of these people actually made excellent teachers and entered into the role with the attitude that it was where God had placed them for the moment. Others were less than exemplary and resented the time spent with "these little white brats."

Another problem was the influence of some of those children who were from non-missions families and who did not come with the values expected of Christians. One instance that resulted in children having to be asked to leave RVA was over spiritualism. Initially the girls began with fairies. They instilled in the younger girls the belief that fairies were real, live beings. Most of the children read fairy stories and recognized fairies as myths, even if they were fun to envision as imaginary things. Soon the little girls were making a house for the fairies in a trunk. All sorts of little furniture pieces were made for the fairies, and the trunk began to look like a miniature doll house. At night the fairies left footprints (painted on by the older girls) showing they had traversed the rooms and used the provided furniture. In general this was accepted as non-threatening and an otherwise inconsequential game. The only trouble came when Grace Shaffer told her little sister Esther what was happening and that it was the older girls who were painting the footprints all over the fairy house, and Esther related this to the other little girls. For a while Esther found herself black-listed among the older girls and some of the little girls who were crushed as their imaginations had led them to accept the possibility of real fairies.

It was not until one of the girls started hearing knocking at night and began communicating with one of our former American presidents that the Lehrers, and subsequently the Downings, became alarmed. Since other girls wanted to talk to former presidents and dead people, a sort of séance was begun. This fell out of the bounds of acceptable behavior at this school created for missionary children, and this girl's family was asked to find another school for their children. This was in the late thirties when spiritualism and séances were in vogue in both England and the United States.

Most of the other behaviors were dealt with on site, and in general the non-missions children fit into the program well and were an asset to the school.

***

In 1941, Ken wrote an article for the mission magazine about two sisters from a non-missionary family who had enrolled at RVA and soon accepted the Lord. At that time there were thirty-five students enrolled. Twelve were from AIM families, three from other missions, and twenty from non-mission homes.

Some children were those of local farmers like the Johansens, whose sons Gordon and Chris were favorites among both staff and students. The Johansens and Downings became friends and often visited back and forth. Gordon recalled Ken and Ivy as both caring and helpful people. Ken and Ivy were especially understanding and compassionate when his brother Chris died while a student at RVA from complications of an injury to his leg that became septic. Gordon ended up marrying Ruth Marie Shaffer, one of the missionary children who later returned to RVA to teach. Tom (Thos) and John (Mac) McNeill's father was a miner and their mother a teacher at Kenton College, a boy's school outside of Nairobi. Their grandfather, John McNeill, was a famous minister from Scotland who served briefly at the well-known Church of the Open Door in Los Angeles. Their uncle, Archie, was a world-renowned evangelist. Both boys have maintained friendships with many former RVA schoolmates. The RVA students looked forward to visits by Thos and Mac's father, Campbell McNeill, as he was a wonderful storyteller and could keep the kids enthralled. Their mother Ruth enjoyed reading to the kids and often acted as a chaperone on the school train as she and her Kenton College students boarded the train before it arrived at Kijabe to pick up the RVA upcountry crowd.

The Roccos came to RVA during the time that Italian men, including their father, Mario, were being interned during World War II. Dorian recalls with warmth that Ken and Ivy accepted them into RVA when most other schools in the British colony would not. Mirella Rocco (now Ricciardi) in her book *African Saga* (pages 89–92) recalls her experience at RVA, mentioning their acceptance and telling of the two happy years they spent there. Oria Rocco, whose husband, Ian Douglas-Hamilton, studies elephants and who runs a lovely lodge in the Samburu area of Kenya, continues to live on the farm in Naivasha. Dorian would sometimes invite one or two of the older boys to go home with him. This was a real treat because they had a unique house, with many of the amenities the missionary children found fascinating. Their mother, Giselle Rocco, was a talented sculptress, so her work was displayed throughout the house, giving the place the aura of a museum or high-end hotel.

Many other non-missionary families have passed through the halls of RVA. The Randalls, the Findleys, and the Aggets all lived down near the original Kijabe railway station, where the first railway line ran below the mission. They walked the three miles uphill each morning for school and then three miles back downhill each afternoon. These miles were through jungle-like terrain in which leopards and other wildlife lived. Their stories, though some were perhaps exaggerated for effect, were listened to with wonder and awe.

Pat, Jean, and Glen Cottar were the children of a famous white hunter, and Glen carried on the hunter tradition until he finally sold his business to Abercrombie and Kent. The Cottar children also had harrowing tales of their father's hunting trips and adventures with animals that entertained and excited the listeners.

Lenita Higgins was known for her beauty, causing many a young male heart to race. It seems a good many of the RVA boys had a crush on her. To this day at RVA reunions, students of that era inquire as to where she may be and what happened to her.

There were many more non-missionary children who passed through the halls of RVA. It is amazing, but not unusual, to find someone who attended school on the slopes of the Great Rift Valley when one travels the world. Immediately, the bonding of shared experience creates a connection that cannot be denied and makes the feeling of family real.

One could go on and on recalling so many of these students who attended RVA in those years when Ken and Ivy were serving. Some have stayed in touch; others have been lost out there in the great big world. It was really a place in time that cannot be duplicated. For most, even for those who experienced tough times as students, the memories have been on balance positive. Friendships created there remain strong, and ties to shared experiences can afford hours of reminiscing.

***

During this time, Ken had to address the continuing problems with changing curricula needs and staff availability to meet those needs. In spite of it all, most students transferring to schools in the United States or Great Britain found that they generally had a good foundation upon which to build.

Added to the problems described above, Ken was also given the responsibility of supervision of the Kijabe Press. This was no small task, as the press was in the era of setting type by hand, requiring careful proofreading because most of the men working there were Kenyans who had a limited ability with English. The Kijabe Press was the only one to serve the growing mission population with Bibles, hymnals, and textbooks in many different languages. The press also published the newsletters for several mission organizations and printed publications such as *Hearing and Doing*, later known as *Inland Africa* for Africa Inland Mission.

Ken was also still in charge of the supervision of schools at Githumu. By 1939, he found that traveling to Githumu in addition to his other responsibilities at Kijabe was too much, and he turned that job over to someone else.

Between 1940 and 1949 he worked with the Kijabe Church. With his fluency in Kikuyu and his knowledge of the people in the region, he was a natural for this job. Over the years from infancy to adulthood, the Downings had made many friends among the local people and were well respected by African and European alike. Knowing the language and being able to converse "like a Kikuyu" was a true asset. However, with RVA and those responsibilities, an aging father who lived on the station, and a growing family, Ken was pressured from many sides.

He was a good-looking man who exuded authority and presence. When Ivy arrived in Kenya and he married her, she was a striking young lady with penetrating eyes, olive complexion, dark brown hair that was pulled straight back in the proverbial missionary bun, and a youthful figure. With the birth of her children she rounded out, making her appear more matronly. She also softened her look with some waves in her hair.

However, both Ken and Ivy immediately instilled in the RVA students the knowledge that no nonsense was going to be tolerated.

Many students lived in fear of incurring their wrath. For those who were compliant and followed rules, life continued much as before and was generally peaceful. But it seemed that all students dreaded the times when someone might incur wrath and everyone got to hear the scolding and ultimate thrashing provided by Ken's leather belt. Although the Lehrers were calmer and not as easily angered, Paul Lehrer did not hesitate to use his rubber hose that was kept in a desk drawer in his office. "Spare the rod and spoil the child" were Scriptures well practiced. (Proverbs 13:24 and 22:15). For most of the children, spankings were accepted as part of growing up and a form of discipline used at home, so most chose to do their best to prevent misdeeds that would elicit the "rod." It also meant that students became adept at subterfuge and sneaking, and one was all right unless caught.

***

Perhaps a short explanation of the school term would help. Early in the life of RVA it was discovered that students who boarded needed to be home with their parents more frequently than the once a year provided by the nine months at school, three months at home system. It was also found that when using the traditional nine/three school year schedule, there was a higher incidence of illness among the students and fatigue among the teachers. With the long distances some had to travel, and with the horrendous road conditions, two weeks at Christmas and shorter holidays were not adequate for the effort necessary to get the children to and from school.

Terms of three months at school and one month home year-round were instituted and found to be much more satisfactory for the boarding situation. A full month of vacation, and a longer time at Christmas, were found to be most satisfactory. The system of year-round school remains at RVA today.

***

From the start, the school was divided into two "houses," Livingstone House and Stanley House, named for the famous explorers David Livingstone and Henry Stanley. The house system was initially used for competitions and eventually expanded to include sports, academics, and discipline. At some point in later years, a black mark system was implemented. Each student started the school term with a clean slate upon which infractions of a rule could result in a black mark being recorded. Rarely, if the "sin" was especially bad, two might be given. When the student had earned ten black marks, he or she was taken before the house meeting and there received a spanking (commonly called a "hiding" by the students) witnessed by all members of their house. Students managing to keep their record from reaching the magic number of ten were rewarded at the end of the school term with a party called a Mutton Roast. Even that name got modified by the students; first to "Mutton Guzzle" and later shortened to "Mutton Guz."

The word mutton got stretched a bit as the meat was not always mutton, but sometimes goat and at other times *kongoni* or other venison shot on the floor of the Rift Valley down below the school. Slabs of meat were skewered on sticks and held over the fire built outside, and ears of corn were roasted in the coals. The wonderful meal was usually topped off with a nice hunk of chocolate cake, roasted marshmallows, or some other sweet.

Students who had not made the list for Mutton Guz had to go to bed early after a meal prepared in the kitchen. Some students report having something like bread and milk, but others said their dinner was not bad, though definitely not as exciting as the Mutton Guz and had to be eaten under the close supervision of a staff member. Those attending the Mutton Guz played games around the bonfire and ended the evening with a hymn sing and prayers.

Competition was keen between the two houses. It was so strong that, in order to keep family harmony, all siblings and family members were placed together in either Livingstone House or Stanley House. Many years later this custom was changed because it was found that it was hard to even out the houses for sports prowess and also academic ability. Besides counting up and giving accolades to the house that had the fewest black marks for rule infractions by all members combined, grades and sports competitions were also tallied.

When Ken and Ivy took over the leadership of RVA, there were only about thirty-five students, so it was not unusual for all to be taken on a hike, for a picnic on the plains, or off to climb one of the local mountains. However, it was the Lehrers who usually planned these outings and acted as sponsors for the day. It was not unusual for a nice long hike that took most of the day to be planned for a Saturday. This kept the students busy and generally out of trouble. However, as with all kids, RVA students could find mischief.

In times past, the whole school could be loaded into the back of a lorry and all taken out on the plains for a day's outing. But, as the school grew, that was no longer possible. It became necessary to take picnics and hikes as houses, and outings were taken as Stanley or Livingstone events.

***

As in the time of his brother Herbert, Kenneth had to manage with the teachers assigned to him. The mission was still sending new missionaries to Kijabe for their language study and, while there, assigning them to teach at RVA. This resulted in some interesting situations where there was a definite mismatch between those willing and able and those who hated teaching, felt uncalled to "white" kids, and rebelled at the expense of the youngsters. The faster they learned their language and passed the first exams the quicker they were relieved of RVA duties. This meant that for some classes there might be two or three teachers in one year. Some who were assigned to teach missionaries' children chose to at least give a year, and some even stayed longer and found they rather liked these kids.

With this unstable teaching staff, Ken and Ivy found themselves filling in the gaps.

The Lehrers were called upon to take up some of the slack at times even though their plates were already overloaded. Sometimes people working in other departments of the mission at Kijabe were asked to come in to teach a class or two. Administration of this fluid situation made for a difficult job for Kenneth.

As the students grew up, missionaries had to decide what to do with their older children. At that time RVA was only educating students through the ninth grade. Parents had to find a home for them in the United States or had to leave Africa themselves in order for their son or daughter to complete high school and college. Some of the older students found themselves teaching younger children and doing a lot of studying on their own. Some went on to schools in Nairobi and took the Senior Cambridge School Certificate exams that equated to a junior college education. A few of the older students were tutored by the Downings and other teachers in order to prepare them for taking the Cambridge exams. Their notification of receiving passing scores was the only high school diploma they would earn.

During this dearth of teachers, Paul Nixon recalls finding time on his hands and not much academic interaction with a teacher as he had passed the eleventh grade but still found himself at RVA. Ken Downing did teach him geometry. He also had an old radio that was not working, and he asked "Nixie" to take it apart, draw a schematic for each part, and show where it fit. Paul found this challenging and educational. He was very glad to find something to do with his time. Eventually he left RVA and went to Edgerton College, an agricultural school in Njoro.

Somewhere in the past, though the timing has been lost, students began calling all adults Pa and Ma. This was never used directly to their faces, but among the children the use of Pa and Ma remains. "Pa Ken," "Ma Ken," "Pa Herb" and "Ma Herb" were not names used in any way other than identification and possibly endearment for most. The Pa and Ma thing was used for all adults living at Kijabe and sometimes beyond. It has been observed that in more recent years among current students this custom has almost vanished. (While gleaning information for this book, the author was interested in the fact that those writing about staff members of that era still referred to them as Pa or Ma something).

Ivy in the meantime was rearing a family and filling in teaching spots when necessary. Daphne was born April 8, 1938. David came along on August 11, 1940, and Dorothy on November 8, 1943.

Incidentally, please note the word "rearing." Ken Downing was a stickler on grammar and correct English usage. As students, RVA children were expected *not* to butcher the King's English. "Animals are raised, children are reared," rings through the mind until this day. Kids were the offspring of goats; children were the offspring of people. Woe betides a student who would mistakenly say, "Grace and me are going," rather than "Grace and I are going." What would Pa Ken say these days to "Me and John did such and such? " or, "Do it for John and I." Horrors! Students can still recall the day Pa Ken attacked the common usage among RVA children of the word "bust" for broken. "I bust my pencil" was how the word was misused in common RVA colloquialism. We were roundly lectured that "bust" was a part of the female anatomy and should not be used to mean broken.

One was not to use the word "hung" for people. Clothes are "hung"; people are "hanged." Although some of the incorrectly used words now appear in the dictionary and are in common usage, Pa Ken would have made heads roll for using them incorrectly. How dare someone use "dove" as the past tense of dive. The correct word is "dived." And, "Chickens lay eggs but people lie down."

Those of us who learned our English usage at RVA are grateful for Ken Downing's unacceptance of poor English usage. (Is "unacceptance" a word, or is it literary license?)

There are many former students who recall incidents with nostalgia and warm thoughts. Anna Verne Smith (now Lee) recalls arriving at school a few weeks late one term because she had been too ill to arrive on time. Ken Downing, whose double major in college was math and physics, was her math teacher and had been "pumping" multiplication tables. When Anna Verne arrived at school, he asked her the answer to seven times eight. She didn't know at that moment, but has never once forgotten since that seven times eight equals fifty-six. Anna Verne remembers Ken as a good math teacher whom she credits with emphasizing the need to memorize tables. Many students credit Ken Downing as being an excellent math teacher. Margaret Andersen (now Schilling) enjoyed math and went on to take algebra and calculus for which she credits Pa Ken and his ability to explain and make math understandable. Lucile Andersen (now Highstreet) on the other hand did not take easily to math. As Ken tried to help her with her struggles, he made the comment, "You'll probably end up majoring in math!"

It was Kenneth Downing and Charlotte Bissett who tutored Lucile for the last two years of high school at RVA so that she was prepared to take her Senior Cambridge School Certificate exams in Nairobi. But it was Ivy who managed to get Lucile a place at the nursing school of Hamilton General Hospital in Hamilton, Ontario, where Ivy had trained. This was a feat for which Lucile has always been grateful, since it did not appear she would be able to fulfill her lifetime dream of become a nurse until Ivy intervened.

***

Ivy Downing filled in resolutely wherever needed during their tenure at RVA. Considering that they took over the school thinking it would just be until Herb and Mildred returned from a year of furlough, they had a lot of adjusting and accepting to do. It was Ivy who tried to find ways to keep these RVA children who were away from home occupied and into constructive ventures. At one time she had a group for some sort of crafts program. Esther Shaffer decided she would melt down old gramophone records to form some sort of artistic objects. Melting the records and getting them shaped did not work out too well, so the project was abandoned. Esther does not recall that Ivy got upset with her for her lack of success, possibly because it was an extracurricular activity.

The Lehrers, who were the homemakers, also tried making the home away from home a pleasant experience. Long hikes and Saturday picnics were common. Saturday evening games nights and Sunday strolls were anticipated, as it meant mingling among the boys and girls, who usually had to adhere to strict segregation. The evening was usually capped off with a treat of some sort like a taffy pull, popcorn, cake, or cookies which always appealed to young sweet teeth.

Ma Lehrer taught the girls how to darn socks, knit, and crochet. Of course, most of the older girls helped the younger ones or brought these skills already learned from home. Pa Lehrer took the older boys hunting on occasion, and they learned how to skin and peg out the hide. Boys and girls alike were kept very busy playing softball, rounders, and tennis for the older kids; hide-and-seek, tag, seesaw, and hopscotch for younger kids.

They also spent hours and hours climbing around like monkeys in two large intricately-branched trees, one on the boys' side and one on the girls'. These iconic trees, scenes of many acted out battles and long-running story lines, were lovingly called "Boys' Green Tree," which still exists after these many years to the delight of grown-up returning alumni, and "Girls' Green Tree," which was where Suswa Dorm now stands. These and other activities occupied time in the afternoons between school and the study hall hour just before supper.

Since the Downing family was quite musical, the study of piano and/or another instruments was almost mandatory. It seems that all students were expected to participate in extra lessons and put in practice time each day. To this day RVA has an excellent instrumental and vocal program.

Teaching piano was another of Ivy's duties, although there were usually several others who also gave piano lessons. Some of her students recall that she was a stickler for counting and accuracy. In her zeal for accurate rhythm, Ivy was known to use a pencil applied to the head of a student to simulate a metronome. Counting while playing was a must, and accurate rhythm imperative.

Penmanship was another of Ivy's "missions." From the third grade on, students were expected to use cursive writing as taught. The Palmer method was the curriculum of choice, so students learned to "use the whole arm," to keep the letters the correct height and evenly spaced. Time was spent each day using the whole arm to make rows and rows of circles and then rows and rows of vertical lines slightly slanted—up and down, up and down, round and round, round and round! Since Ivy had beautiful penmanship, she expected her students to perfect theirs.

There were times when Ivy's rigidity angered students. Always polite kids, they retaliated in other ways. There were times when Ivy found her car, which was usually parked on the RVA circle, with a flat tire. Whether she ever suspected foul play, we do not know.

In hindsight, many students have been grateful for the high standards required under the Kenneth Downings. RVA kids knew correct English usage, and most learned how to spell words both the British and American way. Everyone knew the multiplication tables and how to do the math problems without the use of calculators. They knew how to read and write manuscript and cursive. All students had a good basic understanding of Scripture and had learned many verses and passages by heart before leaving. In general a good education was achieved and the school family became a lasting memory and bond.

***

During one of the critical times of staff shortage, Dr. William Jester and his wife, Daisy, were seconded from their mission in Tanganyika to help out at RVA. William Jester was to act as assistant principal and Daisy, who was a registered nurse, would be the school nurse and in charge of midwifery at the Theodora Hospital at Kijabe. They moved from Tanganyika (Tanzania) with their two children, David and Betty Sue.

World War II was raging, and with the unrest so close to the north in Italian-occupied Ethiopia, RVA had extended one of the school vacations for the sake of insuring safety for the children. It was during one of these extended leaves that Kenneth Downing decided to do some work on his car. During the day he attended to his regular duties, and then at night he worked on the car. Since he had no help, and David Jester, who was fourteen, was bored without school, he offered to help. Although David had little in the way of mechanical skill or knowledge, Kenneth welcomed his assistance. At first Ken had David clean, strip, and sand. Eventually he gave him more responsible jobs, all the while teaching him and giving him valuable mechanical information. Eventually he let David help with the painting. Many nights they worked late installing a new engine and rebuilding a good share of the car and ultimately painting the whole thing. Some nights they worked late making it well after dark when David had to walk home. Kijabe still had wild animals that sometimes prowled around, making the Jesters understandably nervous about David walking home alone.

With the car completed, engine purring, and a slick new paint job, teenager David reveled in the thanks given by Ken for a job well done. David credits this experience with giving him confidence and the courage to try new things. He also learned a lot about mechanics.

The Jesters ended their experience at RVA when asked to escort a very ill missionary home to America. Because they could not travel from the east coast with the war still on, they traveled across Africa through Congo to Angola and on to Portugal. There they took a Portuguese ship that was stopped once by a German submarine. Later an American plane dived down but, seeing it was a Portuguese ship, pulled away at the last minute. David credits his RVA experience, his time with Ken Downing, and the experiences on the way to the

United States for his ability to remain in the United States to complete his high school while his parents went to their next missionary assignment in Nigeria. He did a lot of growing up in a short time.

***

One of the teachers who came to RVA and who made teaching missionary kids her career was Henrietta Propst. She was married to Charles Propst, who had been a student at RVA and later went on to be one of the famous Westervelt Boys. Their daughter Alice recalls her mother's mentioning that she and Kenneth Downing shared the same birthday. Ken called her his twin. At the appropriate time, other missionaries were invited to parties for Henny and Kenny. Alice says her mother hated the name Henny that was inflicted on her by her mother-in-law, Chloe Propst. Ma Henny, as she was known by the students, was beautiful, loving, and gracious, one of the best teachers who ever gave of herself to the children of RVA. She served in the elementary grades until she retired.

Many of the friendships and influences on students continued years after Ken and Ivy moved on to other missionary work. Dorian Rocco recalls not only Pa Ken's teaching him math and physics, but also Ma Ken's efforts at improving his handwriting. In 1945, he was involved with a government project that was preparing for African small land holdings, and found himself working with Wilbur Morrison and Ted Teasdale in surveying the hillsides. He had learned the basics of surveying from Ken Downing and was eternally grateful for the good math basics he learned at RVA. Dorian also recalls Ken meeting with a large gathering of Kikuyu at the beginning of the Mau Mau movement in Naivasha. He, along with Jack Hopcraft, used his very fluent Kikuyu to talk with the people, trying to get them to consider better, non-violent ways to express themselves.

Ken's ability with Kikuyu was recognized by all—Africans, missionaries, and students. Paul Skoda relates that he was confounded that in later years Ken and Ivy were moved to Nyakach which is in Luoland. Although he attempted to learn Luo and was able to use Swahili quite effectively, neither language came as easily for Ken as Kikuyu. Paul wondered at the rationale for moving this man, who could talk like an African in Kikuyu, to a place that was away from his home tribal group. Sometimes we have to accept that there are some things for which we may never have an answer.

During their tenure at RVA Ken and Ivy had increased their little family until they were now five, as Daphne had been joined by David and Dorothy. On September 15, 1945, just thirty days after VJ Day, they sailed on the SS *Abigail Gibbons* from Mombasa, arriving in New York on November 13.

While Ken and Ivy were on the field, Park Street Church in Boston had accepted Ken as a supported member. It was a blessing to have such a missions-minded church helping with their support. On October 4, 1946, Ken was ordained by Park Street Church. During its annual missions conference, Ken and Ivy had a chance to tell about their work in Kenya and to become acquainted with many in their new church home.

On December 20, 1946, Ken and Ivy and their children, along with Herbert and Mildred and their children, boarded the SS *Marine Carp* for their return to Kenya.

The time had come for Acting Principal Kenneth Downing to turn over the responsibilities of the Rift Valley Academy back to Principal Herbert Downing. The short assignment had lasted ten years. He could now get back into the work for which he had originally come back to Kenya.

11.

The Long Furlough: Herbert and Mildred 1937–1947

Herbert and Mildred's long absence from RVA had begun when they and their children, Gayle, age six, and Glenn, age three, sailed from Mombasa on the SS *West Isleta* on October 9, 1937, traveling via Capetown to New York. They arrived in New York on November 13. Also traveling with them was a little stowaway who was due to be born very shortly. Although the French captain was concerned that the baby might make an appearance before landing, Edwin Lee graciously waited until November 24 to make his appearance.

Years later, Ed received this letter from Mildred regarding his birth.

I've been remembering bringing you from Africa around "The Cape of Good Hope" to the United States...Edwin Lee Downing— born in New Concord, Ohio at an "Old Folks Home" on November 24, 1937, 7:15 PM, the night before Thanksgiving. Your Dad tried to give me a "whiff" of chloroform and got it himself and he slid under the bed. When I tried to check on him Dr. Herbert Bain assured me he was safe and added "You have a job to do." Since you had not even a diaper—friends gave the needed supplies. I had knitted outfits for later—can you imagine having a baby without all the medical checks they have here?! Anyway—you're here—a miracle—and a cause for Thanksgiving for me. I do thank the Lord for you—and the family He has given you.

Mildred sent this story to Ed after she was widowed in 1986. Ed called her almost every Sunday evening, and that may have prompted her reminiscing about the child she called her "miracle baby." Father Downing had prayed and then received God's answer about their taking a furlough at a time that Mildred was eight months pregnant and there was no money for traveling. He arrived at their door to assure them that it was right for them to go. So they went to Mombasa, where Herbert found tickets for passage and they boarded a French freighter headed to New York. Myrtle Zafke, RN, also traveled with them and no doubt would have been an excellent midwife in case of early labor and delivery. Had that happened Ed could have chosen French citizenship when he came of age. Mildred had had no prenatal care and the only physician available in New Concord, Ohio, was a GP. The only medical facility was the "Old Folks Home." There were many eager "grandmas" ready to hold and rock a new born any time he whimpered or had a gas pain. Mildred never quite forgave them for "spoiling" her baby at such an early age!

***

The year 1937 found the United States in hard economic times and the Downings were not without their monetary concerns. Apparently the problems were so great that some of the relatives wanted to adopt little Eddie. As with most children, this kind of information was used to trigger needling and sometimes fights. Glenn used to love pointing out to Eddie Lee that he had just about been given away and could have had the surname Shaner, although there is no evidence that Herb and Mildred even considered giving up their son. Eddie Lee's response was, "They didn't want you! And I was cute and friendly!"

The family lived in New Concord, Ohio, where Mildred's father was the Presbyterian minister and where Muskingum College was located. Both Herb and Mildred had ties to the college, and Herb got a maintenance job on campus. Here his multiple talents were used. A quote of Herb's, which many working with him through the years heard over and over was "The gift of the man maketh room for him." He was one gifted man! He also worked as a lab assistant at Muskingum College and coordinator of the new Civil Aeronautics Administration's pilot training program on campus. Herb drove an old 1930 Chevrolet to get around to his jobs, an automobile that often used his mechanical talents to keep running.

Later Herbert was able to find work teaching ground school for pilots. The job was far enough away that he was only able to come home on weekends. He wore an officer's uniform but had no bars for rank. He also did the same type of training for Bowling Green State University, Bowling Green, Ohio. While working at the university, he attended classes and completed his master's degree in education. Teaching ground school inspired him to learn how to actually fly an airplane, so he took flying lessons. There was no idle time on his hands.

Herbert took on pastoring at a little church in a farm community. The family now became farmers, witnessed calves being born, and learned to drive tractors and how to pitch hay. There were not many vacations or fun trips during those days, but there were several trips to conferences at Winona Lake.

***

On April 18, 1942, Ruth Ann was born at Bethesda Hospital in Zanesville, Ohio, the nearest hospital to New Concord. Now, besides having a baby, three children, and a home to keep, Mildred taught math at Muskingum College. Herbert was away so much of the time working at the airport during the week and coming home weekends, that Mildred later told Ruth Ann that she became a real mama's girl because her dad seemed to be a strange guy coming around every once in a while. Her siblings called her a pain because she cried so much, apparently from earaches. Ruth Ann's retort was that the family didn't appreciate the gift that their parents gave them when they brought her home from the hospital.

They did have visitors though. One of the visitors Ed recalls well is Roy David Shaffer, who arrived looking smart in his military uniform, and his sister Ruth Marie, who was teaching at Wheaton Academy, the boarding high school connected to Wheaton College. They took Ed to the college to show him the campus, which was very impressive to this young man. Several years later Ed would meet his wife, Lois, on the campus of Wheaton where they were both students.

***

Lois Epp grew up in the Belgian Congo, where her parents were missionaries under Africa Inland Mission. Congo children attended Rethy Academy for their education. As often happens at boarding schools, one child gets chicken pox, measles, or any number of communicable diseases, and soon the illness makes the rounds. Lois's best friend, Mary Lee, got an undiagnosed fever and was evacuated to Kulava Hospital in Uganda, where Ted and Peter Williams were the doctors. She died there two weeks later of rheumatic fever. Hearing the news of their daughter's illness and death via ham radio, this girl's parents rushed hundreds of miles to attend her funeral.

Two weeks after this incident, Lois came down with a fever that closely resembled that of her friend. She also had excruciating pain in her right abdomen. So closely following the other death, Lois's illness caused great alarm, and Herb and Muriel Cook at Rethy quickly packed Lois up to go to Kulava since the William brothers were the closest medical doctors. Eleven-year-old Lois was sure she was going to die, just as her friend had done.

At Kulava, Drs. Ted and Peter removed her appendix during an exploratory laparoscopy, thinking the pain might be due to appendicitis, but found nothing unusual there. The Epps also heard the news via ham radio and rushed through blinding rain and difficult road conditions, praying they would arrive in time to see their daughter alive.

Lois did not die, but spent her sixth grade year in bed, trying to keep up with studies, playing paper dolls for whom she constructed large wardrobes, and reading and memorizing Scriptures. Her pain persisted even though each new antibiotic that arrived at the hospital was tried. There would be temporary relief, and then the old pain and fever would return. The doctors were baffled, so her grandparents in the United States made arrangements for Lois to enter Illinois Research Hospital. The Epps began to close down their work in preparation for making the journey to the United States. While this was going on Lois was taken to Oicha, Belgian Congo, to stay with Dr. Carl and Mrs. Becker since the Williams were in England on furlough.

Dr. Becker did diathermy treatments because this seemed to relieve the pain in her side. He noticed a red spot that remained over her right kidney. He recalled seeing a Belgian patient with a similar condition, so lanced and drained the area, and within days Lois was up and relearning to use her muscles for walking. He diagnosed it as a perinephric abscess. Needless to say her parents were delighted, and the trip to Illinois Research was cancelled. Twenty-one years later Lois Rachel Epp married Edwin Lee Downing.

Lois has always credited Dr. Carl Becker with saving her life. During Ed's last year of medical school, Dr. Becker went to Philadelphia to speak at a Christian Medical society meeting that

Lois and Ed attended. It was there that Dr. Becker told them that it was grandfather Lee Downing who had persuaded him to leave a busy Pennsylvania medical practice to become a missionary doctor. He established the medical center at Oicha, Belgian Congo, taught himself to do the many types of surgery needed, as he had been trained in homeopathic medicine, and later established a hospital at Nyankunde, Zaire, with a consortium of five other missions.

Throughout Africa Inland Mission, the name Dr. Carl Becker is still remembered as an exceptional physician and a true servant of God.

***

In 1945 the Kenneth Downings left Kenya for a furlough and persuaded Herbert and his family that it was time to return to Kenya and resume the principalship of RVA. The miracle of the passage home from Mombasa in 1937 had resulted in the Herb Downings' being required to repay the mission for their passage. At least they had been able to get home, so they still considered it a blessing that the way had been provided, even though it was sort of a temporary miracle and they eventually had to pay back the money to AIM.

Ken's tenure as acting principal had turned out to be ten years rather than the normal one year. But now the war was over, and travel was considered safe. Ken was sure the school was waiting for Herb's leadership. Although Ken did not have the authority of the Field Council to make assignments, and Herbert knew that he and Mildred could be assigned to African work, they began making preparations to get back to Kenya. This furlough had been long and hard, but they had learned many lessons, both spiritually and academically, that would stand them in good stead in the future.

In December both Downing families, along with many other missionaries who had been waiting, delayed by the war, left New York on the MV *Marine Carp*. They arrived in Mombasa on January 21, 1947.

12.

Life After RVA: Ken and Ivy

Even while serving as principal at RVA, Ken had been busy with the African work, school supervision, Kijabe Press, and translation of Scriptures into Kikuyu.

One time in 1938, Ken wrote for the mission newsletter *Kenya Views* about a meeting that was held at Siyabei (now spelled Siapei on maps). Because of the shortage of manpower, the station was without missionaries. A Kikuyu evangelist had accompanied Ken to Siyabei, which is in the heart of Maasai land, and delivered a powerful message using Jonah as his topic. He likened the church at Siyabei to Jonah, who had left the deck of the ship and gone down into the hold to sleep. The ship was fine, but the man was not. The church at Siyabei was fine, but the workers there had gone below to sleep. At the end of the sermon, several stepped forward having recognized themselves as those who had "gone below to sleep." Incidents like this were not infrequent as Ken went about his job of supervising the schools and churches.

In 1940, Ken and Ivy went to Congo, taking Father Downing along as they felt the lower altitude and change would be good for him. Lee had never been to Congo by car, so this was a whole new experience for him. There were no cars or roads in Central Africa when he went in the early days. Traveling along at such a high speed, probably thirty to forty miles per hour, seemed like sailing to a man who had walked or ridden a bicycle wherever he went. Experiencing the differences in the terrain, from grasslands through elephant grass and rain forests, was met with wonder.

The people in Congo were delighted to have Lee Downing visit their field, as his reputation was legendary. Having been so influential in Kenya and honored as such a man of God, Lee was revered. Having that type of recognition bothered Lee, as he was basically a very humble man.

Ivy, "being great with child," was expecting her second baby. Dr. Carl Becker at Oicha delivered David William on August 11, 1940.

Back home again at Kijabe, Ken's ability with the Kikuyu language was being used in Bible translation, and in 1942 he was able to hand over the completed translation of Hosea to the United Kikuyu Language Committee. The first draft of Hosea had been done by Fred McKenrick; now Ken edited it and made necessary revisions.

Having become increasingly frail, Father Downing died on May 13, 1942. Although he had been in failing health for some time, losing him was a blow not only to the Downing family but also to the greater missions family and the African community. Lee Downing's reputation was immense and known throughout central Africa and the United States. He was greatly missed by many, and his influence was felt for years to come. One missionary child reflected her mother's sentiments by saying, "My mother thought the Downings walked on water!"

The following is an excerpt from the July–August 1942 *Inland Africa*:

"So another one of the foundations stones upon which the vast work of the Africa Inland Mission was built on earth has left for higher service. We honor his memory and thank God upon every remembrance of him."

Three years after Father Downing's death, Ken and Ivy with their three children, Daphne, David, and Dottie, left for furlough on the SS *Abigail Gibbons,* sailing from Mombasa. This was the official end to Ken's temporary assignment as interim principal of RVA. On their return, Ken was assigned to supervision of the Kijabe Church, among other responsibilities. He taught at Moffatt Bible School for four months, and although he was already able to converse quite well, he began the formal study of Kiswahili. By June he was also assigned the supervision of the printing press.

In June of 1948, he was appointed general secretary of the Africa Inland Church. This was the start of a growing list of increasingly important offices and responsibilities he was asked to fill over the next forty years.

That December, Ken and Ivy welcomed a belated Christmas present: Lee Herbert Downing, named for his grandfather and uncle, was born at the Maia Carberry Nursing Home in Nairobi on December 26, 1948.

In July 1949, Ken and Ivy moved to Githumu, a place where his fluency in Kikuyu was a definite asset. The family now included Daphne, David, Dottie, and Lee.

The move back to Githumu required another adjustment, that of sending their own children to boarding school. As children, Ken and Herb had attended RVA as day students, living at home and walking to school (with the exception of the one school term when Herbert boarded). Ken had served as principal and lived on site, so until the move to Githumu, his children were also day students. Now, at Githumu, although it was one of the closer stations, it was still too far for a daily commute. Having to put the children in boarding school gave Ken and Ivy new empathy for those parents who had suffered sending their children away to board in order to be educated. However, they could both thank God for the school since it avoided the necessity of leaving their children in the United States or finding another way to educate their youngsters. Many other missions, without the facility of a school like RVA, had expected children to be left in the home country when they became school age. Daphne and David became boarding students at RVA and found the change from day to boarding didn't cause major trauma. Again Ken and Ivy were grateful for the decision to have RVA on a rotation of three months of school, one month at home, year round. They had experienced this as teachers and appreciated the more frequent breaks; now they understood the situation from the parents' viewpoint.

Several significant events now occurred in the Downing family. They welcomed Victor Kenneth, on May 10, 1950, at the Alice Beaton Hospital in Nairobi. That same year, Ken was appointed field council secretary. In 1951, Ken was appointed education secretary for the Kenya Field. This was the group in charge of the African schools run by Africa Inland Mission.

In April of 1951, Ken and Ivy were transferred to Nyakach, which is located on a plateau overlooking Lake Victoria and the city of Kisumu. From Nyakach Ken was to supervise AIM schools in Central Nyanza, the area on the Kenya side of the Lake Victoria region. He, along with John Allen, supervised the Luo schools.

Life at Nyakach was somewhat primitive in that there was no main line electricity, running water, or telephones. By the late 1950s, it became necessary to communicate over the AIM mission network with single sideboard short-wave radio. Every morning at 7:30 stations without telephone service called into Nairobi via the radio. Someone in Nairobi went through the list of every station, which sometimes was thirty or more, taking messages or giving messages. The stations took their turns speaking with other stations. Sometimes the caller would just reply "no traffic," or it might be "one or two messages," in which case the operator would take the messages and see that they were passed on. For those in remote areas, this radio contact was their lifeline to civilization. Since it was radio communication, the common calls of "Roger" and "over" created the nickname among the overhearing Africans of the "over-over."

Before breakfast at Nyakach, Ken and Ivy checked in and then usually listened to the whole call-up because one never knew what news they might hear or what message someone had for them. Emergency calls might be for a plane to transport someone very ill, cattle raids in Lokori, or a new baby born to a missionary family.

It was on the "over-over" some years later that Ken announced the engagement of Dottie to Jonathan Hildebrandt in 1973. This announcement brought a round of congratulations, again via the "over-over." This was very much the general party line where everyone could listen in and no secret could be kept.

Ivy was known for her excellent cooking and meals presented with a flair. Her kitchen at Nyakach was a good size, but had limited natural light. Evening meals were especially difficult as Ken preferred not to turn on the generator until 7:00 p.m., and sunset was close to 6:00 p.m. That meant using a small kerosene lantern that produced minimal light. Although Ivy had kitchen help for clean-up and perhaps vegetable preparation such as shelling peas, she did the cooking herself. The evening meal was a light supper because the big meal of the day was at noon or one o'clock. Having house help was common and necessary among missionaries, as every task was multiplied by the conditions. There were no dishwashers, vacuum cleaners, automatic washing machines and dryers, or other conveniences that we in the United States consider necessities. Floors were rough wood, cement, or even dirt.

At Nyakach the bathroom was only a room where a tub had been constructed out of concrete. Although a finishing coat of cement had been added, it was still quite rough and not conducive to sliding in and out. Perhaps it could be better described as the perfect exfoliation treatment for one's posterior. It was several years before Ken and Ivy got an indoor toilet and did not have to hike to the outhouse where one found the proverbial "long-drop."

The Downings' long-drop was a short walk of about forty feet away from the main house. A two-seater had been constructed, with one higher than the other, making it possible for an adult or a child to sit in comfort. The "soil stack" or ventilation system devised by Ken kept it virtually odor-free and fly-proof. There was reading material provided as well as a linoleum floor for easier cleaning. A washstand with a basin and water was provided along with clean towels. Actually, it was commended by many visiting missionaries as "the nicest out-house in Kenya."

The house at Nyakach had been built by Herbert Innis in 1911 out of fieldstone and cemented together, resulting in very thick walls. The windows were small, allowing for very little light. Ceilings were Kavirondo reed mats that were about seven feet by seven feet and hung on the rafters. They did serve to keep the rodents and their droppings from falling through. Eventually the mats disappeared when corrugated iron replaced the thick, thatched roof, making the rooms a bit lighter. One of the best things about this house was the wonderful screened porch that extended down the side of the building. The porch was right on the edge of the Nyakach Plateau and looked over the Sondu River Valley, with a magnificent view of Lake Victoria. If the light was just right, one could even see the small fishing boats on the lake.

It was on this porch that Ivy faithfully served afternoon tea. The wonderful Kenya tea was accompanied by some of Ivy's delicious confections. Sitting out on the porch, one could watch the sunset out over the Sondu Valley and Lake Victoria. After dark one could see the lights of Kisumu, the town by the lake. After tea, Ivy went into the kitchen to prepare the light supper that would be served about 7:30.

Ivy planted a small garden, which helped supply her kitchen. Her prize was a small grove of mulberry trees that produced wonderful fruit from which she made pies, jams, and jellies. Those trees were guarded and harvested with great care.

Keeping cars running was a constant chore for most missionaries, as the roads were not conducive to automobile maintenance. A clever pit was constructed out of field–stone and cement in the side of the plateau, making it easy for Ken to drive his car right onto the tracks. By walking down a few steps he was able to walk under his car to work on it.

Keeping the cars running was only one of the fix-it jobs necessary. Fortunately, Ken was a gifted *fundi,* and able to fix just about anything, despite the fact that he did not own a variety of power tools and gadgets. His son-in-law Jonathan Hildebrandt told the following story about him.

"Ken could do some amazing repairs. One small example among many was the repair of a Sunbeam toaster that the family brought back from furlough in Canada in 1956. After many years of service (being only used in the evenings when the generator was on) it broke. Most people would have tossed it out and bought a new one, but Ken carefully disassembled it, cracking one of the Bakelite handles in the process, repaired the electrical fault, and put it back together, carefully drilling holes in the Bakelite and inserting two screws, so that you would hardly know it was broken." That toaster is still being used in the Hildebrandt household at their retirement home in Florida. Jonathan states it is a very special toaster that slowly lowers the bread, toasts it perfectly, and then slowly pushes the toast up again.

In May of 1953 Ken was made acting field director and gave up the job of field council secretary and the Africa Inland Church general secretary. In June of that year RVA needed homemakers for a year, so Ken and Ivy returned to RVA, this time in a whole new capacity. During the school terms they were dormitory supervisors, but at the school breaks they went back to Nyakach to carry on the work there. Being dorm parents was another new experience for Ken and Ivy. Now Ken had been administrator, teacher, parent, and homemaker at RVA.

In 1953 when the British colonial government wanted to put Jomo Kenyatta on trial for his participation in the Mau Mau movement, Ken was asked if he would be the official English-to-Kikuyu interpreter for Mzee Kenyatta. Although Kenyatta spoke English well, having studied in England, the government wanted to be sure he understood exactly what was being said. Ken declined the appointment because he felt that his participation could damage his ministry with the Kikuyu and other Africans if they perceived he was controlled by the colonial government. A local white farmer, who was not nearly as fluent with Kikuyu, had a limited vocabulary, and had poor grammar, was hired.

Visiting at stations and living among the local people put Ken in a position to hear and feel the unrest that was gathering. The Mau Mau movement was primarily among the Kikuyu people, and Githumu was right in the center of this group. Although it was about June of 1952 when the Mau Mau movement became evident with acts of violence, it had been smoldering for several years. Erik Barnett wrote this explanation of the background of Mau Mau in the June 1954 *Inland Africa,* under the title "Reevaluation through Persecution": *The grievances leading to this unrest centered around land, race discrimination, better wages, proper housing, political equality, education, a fear by some that the old customs would be lost, and a number of similar problems.*

The British colonial government was aware of the problems and had been working toward solving them. However, for those who were militant Mau Mau, the solutions were not coming fast enough to suit them. There seemed to be a fear that by waiting, their clout would be diluted, and their goal of driving out the white man and everything to do with Christianity would fail.

Erik Barnett, who was the field director in Kenya, had written this about the political situation festering in Kenya in the January–February 1953 issue of *Inland Africa*:

An assessment of the political situation in Kenya is exceedingly difficult owing to the changes from day to day in the underground activity of the subversive movements causing disturbances. A movement called the Mau Mau, having as its objective the ousting of the British government in Kenya and its promoting of interests of non-Africans is responsible for the situation. The reason stated is that the white people have stolen much of the Africans' land and that, in order to get this back, the British Government and all that it stands for must be removed.

Missions have become a target of the Mau Mau because of their teaching that one should obey the powers that be, for they are ordained of God. Mission adherents are for law and order. The Mau Mau movement repudiates Jesus and uses the name of its leader, Jomo, in the place of Jesus, and the name of Mumbi, the fabled mother of the Agikuyu people, in the place of the Holy Spirit. A hymnbook using Christian hymn tunes has been published by the Mau Mau with these changes in it.

It appears now that this subversive movement intends to attain its objective by civil disobedience, intimidating Africans loyal to Government, and further, to pillage European farms, murdering anyone it feels uncooperative, both white and black. The aim of all of the lawlessness is to cause embarrassment to the Government and fear to the white population in hopes that they will withdraw from the country. Africans initiated into the secret society of the Mau Mau must take oaths, which to the heathen are particularly binding. These oaths bind the partakers to blind obedience to all orders that are issued by the Mau Mau.

Up to this present time, about one hundred Africans have been murdered, including two senior chiefs. These Africans were murdered because of their non-cooperation with the Mau Mau movement. A few European settlers have been attacked, and some European farmers have lost large numbers of stock through slaughter and mutilation.

The British government declared a state of emergency and sent troops to assist the local government. Kijabe and Githumu had troops, called the Home Guard, assigned, and night patrols were organized for the protection of Africans and whites alike. Fortunately no missionaries or missionary children died in these troublesome days, but the African Christian church and its adherents suffered a lot.

In the March–April 1956 issue of *Inland Africa* Ken wrote about a young man named Kiarie who had been a general in the Mau Mau movement. He was called the School Boy General because as a very young boy he had taken the Mau Mau oath and been placed as a "general" over an armed gang. They stayed in the dense forests above the Rift Valley and made raids on the communities below. One of these communities was Lari, where a massacre occurred, hundreds were brutally murdered, and the village was totally destroyed by fire.

On one of their raids, the gang had been broken up and Kiarie captured. Ironically he had been placed in a detention camp under Headman Paulo's Home Guard Post at Kijabe. Paulo and his men were Christians and daily witnessed to their detainees. It was due to these men's faithfulness and witness that Kiarie finally broke out of his oath and gave his life to the Lord.

As usually happens when the Church is under persecution, it became stronger and the adherents more deeply committed. The majority of Christian leaders stood firm even though many suffered the loss of their lives, family, and property. Ironically, Kenya today is predominantly a Christian country, and the work of missions continues to thrive.

13.

Herbert and Mildred: Rift Valley Academy, 1947–1964

When Herbert and Mildred arrived in New York the day before they were to sail for Kenya in 1947, they discovered that the AIM home office had failed to book passage for Gayle. Tickets were on hand for Herbert, Mildred, Glenn, Eddie Lee, and baby Ruth Ann. But, because she was fifteen and too old for RVA, AIM had assumed that Gayle would be left in the States to complete high school and then go on to college. After pulling some strings and making last–minute adjustments, Herb got Gayle aboard, where she would bunk in sick bay with her aunt Ivy and cousins. Since this was a troopship, accommodations bunked men in one area and women in another, so she did not think sleeping in sick bay was a bad option. At least she had not been left behind and would be with her family a few more years.

It appeared to be a foregone conclusion that Herbert and Mildred would take over responsibilities at RVA now that they were back in Kenya. The years since they left had changed the school, but not tremendously. The war and limitations on travel had kept the school at about forty in attendance, with many of those students the children of non-missionary families.

With Gayle and several others almost to the age when RVA could no longer provide for their education, Herb began considering making RVA a full high school. Yes, others had completed their work at RVA, but they had needed to go into Nairobi to sit for the Cambridge exams in order to have verification of completion. Now it was time for RVA to offer its own diploma. One student, Paul Smith, was the first one to receive an RVA high school diploma in 1949. The following year, 1950, there were four, including Herb's own daughter Gayle.

***

More and more missionaries were arriving to serve in Kenya, Tanganyika, and Uganda under AIM. There were also other missions that were growing, and with this boom, RVA began a rapid growth. It soon became apparent that the number of "outsiders" would have to be

Mildred teaching: Esther Shaffer, Gloria Kitts, Gayle Downing, Gerald Morrison, Donald Kirkpatrick, Harold LaFont, David Amtutz

limited to make room for missionary children. The philosophy was that AIM children were first, other missions second, and non-missions third, if there was room. Along with these changes came an important one for RVA: missionaries were going to Kenya specifically to teach at RVA. Having a more stable and consistent pool of teachers made a tremendous difference in the planning for classes and duties necessary for running such an operation.

In December 1946, Clara Barrett and Ruth Marie Shaffer (now Johansen) arrived to teach at RVA. Clara was a trained librarian, but found herself in a primary classroom because that is where she was needed. While she taught in the primary grades at RVA, she gave piano lessons. As librarian, she turned the library into a first–class collection. After thirty-five years of service, she retired in 1981 and moved to the AIM retirement center in Clermont, Florida. In March 1986, she was flown back out to Kijabe for dedication of RVA's newly constructed library, named the Clara Barrett Library.

Ruth Marie, on the other hand, taught grades four through six and home economics in the high school. Then she married her RVA school sweetheart, Gordon Johansen, in 1948, and later they moved to his family's coffee and sisal farm near Machakos.

Ruth Marie had grown up in Kenya as the daughter of Roy and Ruth Shaffer, who worked among the Maasai, so living in Kenya was not a major adjustment for her. The harder adjustment had been going to the States for her higher education. But, during that time Ruth Marie used to visit with the Downings, then at Bowling Green, Ohio. Being with people from "home" was a comfort, and she was always made to feel welcome. Those experiences were important to a girl so far from home and family. She specifically recalls little Eddie Lee perching himself on her shoulders and singing his little heart out as she played the piano. But best of all, she got to help care for newborn Ruth Ann, who had joined the family during that time. So in her new role as a settler's wife, after marrying Gordon, she kept in close touch with Downings, but RVA lost her as a teacher.

This was when her brother, Roy Shaffer and his wife, Betty, came out to the field and were both assigned to teach at RVA. They also house-parented a dorm of fourteen rambunctious boys in the old red brick house Lee Downing built for Blanche.

Some of the other new RVA teachers, like Minda Graff, came to the RVA staff in other ways. Minda was a registered nurse who arrived in Kenya assigned to work at the Theodora Hospital at Kijabe under the supervision of Dr. Jim Propst. Initially she was assigned to learn Swahili, the trade language of Kenya. The plan was for her to work at Kijabe while learning language and the ropes, and then to go out to the villages in more remote places. Minda was supposed to be headed to Mulango where Harman Nixon would be her mentor and help her with language study and acculturation.

As with many new missionaries, Minda went to the Herb Downings' for afternoon tea. There she was asked if she would consider teaching biology and serving as school nurse for RVA while doing language study. Minda always laughed about her assignment as a school nurse. She said, "I started out with a bottle of aspirin." The students joked that Ma Graff would send them off to bed "with an aspirin and a big jug of water to drink." Soon after completing her

**Roy Shaffer with a class: Liz Guldseth, Lois Teasdale,
Daphne Downing, Edwin Downing, Will Danielson**

stint at Kijabe, Minda moved on to Mulango to begin her assignment.
Shortly after she moved there, she heard that Myrtle Zaffke, another
nurse, was back and would be coming to take her place. Minda wrote
Erik Barnett, who was the field director, stating that she was willing
to go back to RVA. Her request was granted for one term. That term
was to last for fourteen years. Now RVA had its first official school
nurse. Although Ivy Downing was a registered nurse, her job had not
specifically been as school nurse. While carrying out the school nurse
responsibilities, Minda was pressed into service in the school office,
which was temporarily located in the Downing home. She and Clara
also had a dorm of fifteen or sixteen little boys to mother and care for.
Staff members at RVA learned to flex and adjust to whatever the needs
happened to be. When she retired, Minda, who had been a Navy nurse,
moved to a military retirement community in northern California.

For the most part working with missionaries' children had finally
been accepted by home churches as a form of mission service. With
the growing population of students, it was necessary to increase the
number of teachers and staff.

Although we do not know whether they came with the primary purpose of teaching at RVA, there were others, not already mentioned, who came during the 1950s and '60s who served for their whole career or for many years. Among them were Verity Coder, Bob and Dottie Giddings, Alan Hovingh, Ina Reed, Gladys Bellinger, Sam and Kay Senoff, Faye Leitch, Judy Cooke, Shirley Lasse, Trumball "Si" and Mary Simmons, Geraldine Stocum, Glenden and Greta Rae, and Dorothy White. Others came after being evacuated from Congo, and

Kinyanjui (Downing's house helper) brings his family to visit

others came for a few years to help out. (There may have been others not listed. Please forgive the author if your name is missing.)

***

In about 1950, during one of the school vacations, Mildred decided she would go to Aja, Congo, to visit their good friends Harold and Jane Amstutz. Herbert did not feel that he could leave RVA because there were just too many maintenance jobs needing to be done. It was decided that Gayle and Eddie Lee would stay with Herbert, while Glenn and Ruth Ann went with Mildred. Gayle was about eighteen at the time and Eddie Lee about thirteen.

One of the days while Mildred was gone, Herbert decided to visit a childhood friend who was now a chief. It was a long ride from Kijabe over some awful roads, but they finally reached Chief Kala's village. The two men were very happy, to see each other and they

Herbert on safari with Dr. Jim Propst.
Here he mends or creates a part for an incapacitated vehicle.

talked and talked in Kikuyu, which neither Gayle nor Eddie Lee could understand. What they could understand was that their father was completely at ease and happy in this environment. All day long the visiting went on, with the chief frequently looking out his window in order not to miss anything going on.

The chief gave Eddie Lee a dozen eggs, which he used to make eggnog every day for a week. Later Herbert told Gayle and Eddie Lee that Chief Kala had been one of Father Downing's first students. On the way home, Herbert told his two children about going by bicycle with his father to visit mission stations. As Herbert told the stories of his father, Eddie Lee and Gayle wished they had known their grandfather. However, Eddie Lee did get the idea that the long bicycle rides had not been one of Herb's favorite activities.

Eddie Lee's appreciation for his father's great respect for the Africans and their respect for him was confirmed once again that day as they visited in the chief's house. It also made Eddie Lee appreciate the work done by his grandfather and those who brought education to these people. He felt a great pride in his heritage as a Downing, the son of Herbert and grandson of Lee.

**

There were changes happening in Kenya. Rumblings of unrest and demands for freedom from British rule began to fester below the surface. As Ken was experiencing elsewhere, the Africans, especially the Kikuyu tribe, felt disenfranchised by the white man who had come to take over their land. In the "white highlands" of Kenya, huge plots of land had been granted for agriculture to the foreign settlers. Land, to the African, is more than his livelihood: it holds a certain mystical connection with his ancestry and spirit. Although the white farmers employed many Africans to work their farms, and most took good care of their help, there remained an elitism and racism that festered and rankled. The attitude among some was that Africans were inferior intellectually and required supervision and handling. Even many missionaries held these assumptions and treated the black population as children needing discipline and guidance. As the missionaries made converts to Christianity, and as these people went to school, it became evident that they were very capable of learning and were not intellectually inferior. Now, the goal of AIM and most other missions became to work toward the time when the missionaries could turn over leadership and let the local people take over.

The clamor for education resulted in mixed blessings when some Africans found that those with an education were able to find work that paid better than the menial farm labor. Non-mission schools began to spring up, becoming breeding grounds for discontent and promoting "the movement."

The undercurrent of unrest continued to bubble, while secret meetings and rituals requiring blood oaths evolved into the movement called Mau Mau. In general those who joined the movement were not those who were educated and who had found a place in the more modern Kenya, but those who were poor and had not been assimilated into the new culture. And there were some who saw in this upheaval a way to achieve their own ends of power and wealth. The oaths included a pledge to trick the white man and to kill if necessary. This was to include those loyal to the British crown and all Christians, because they were considered loyalists as well.

The rumblings that had been simmering since 1948 had become violent by 1952. The first victim was Chief Waruhiu, a man loyal to the colonial government. Next was a family of three who were brutally murdered and dismembered. By February 1953, 9 Europeans, 3 Indians, 177 Kikuyu, and 13 other Africans had been killed. Those killed were loyal to the government and/or Christians. A Christian was considered loyal to the white man because he had embraced the white man's religion and rejected some of the tribal customs, such as female circumcision. Another irritation was the *kipandi*, a booklet of identification that all were required to carry, black or white. Having a *kipandi* was rather like a social security number, making it possible for the government to tax. The question of where the name of Mau Mau came from has resulted in many theories and possibilities, but all agree it was not a complimentary term. Those in the movement preferred to call it "The Movement."

On October 21, 1952, Jomo Kenyatta, who was alleged to be the instigator and leader, was arrested. Immediately, Sir Evelyn Baring, the governor, proclaimed a state of emergency in Kenya. A missionary at Kijabe, Wellesley Devitt (commonly known as Welles), was asked to be the local "pass officer," the one who would monitor the movements of the people with the use of their *kipandis*. Welles, who had served with the British army in the King's African Rifles as a chaplain in World War II, was well respected by both the local Africans and the British government and seemed a perfect one for this job. Although his popularity was useful for the government and missions, he soon became a wanted man by the Mau Mau and lived in constant danger. A group of African soldiers called The Home Guard was deployed to Kijabe to help with the security.

***

In the midst of all this trouble, it came time for the Downings to leave for furlough. In June of 1952, after Glenn graduated, they left Kenya. This time they flew to London and then sailed on the SS *Liberté* to New York, arriving there on June 10.

During this furlough, John Martin joined the family on March 20, 1953, in Ohio. Although Martin was less than a year old, they felt that with Kenya in such troubled times, they needed to be back at RVA. Leaving Gayle and Glenn in the States was hard, but it was time for them to be in college. Herbert and Mildred, Eddie Lee, Ruth Ann, and Martin were back in Kenya on April 25 of 1954.

While they were away, the Mau Mau problems had escalated, and they came back to find the scene quite different than when they had left. For one thing their house was gone and with it many of their earthly possessions, including baby pictures and wedding pictures, as well as other precious mementos. Their belongings that had been stored in the attic awaiting their return were all gone.

While the Downings were on furlough, the Hollenbeck family was living in the Downing's house. This was a common thing at Kijabe. When one family left for furlough someone else moved in. There was always a constant shuffling of housing.

Jim Hollenbeck's forte was instrumental music, and he was responsible for band, orchestra, and choral music. Although Herb already had an orchestra going, Jim soon had the RVA students formed into a marching band that was worthy of any stateside school.

Vivian Hollenbeck took on the task of the school laundry. With the growing population of students, now over ninety, the laundry had become a major undertaking. There were mountains of dirty clothes each week. Even though she had African help, it required supervision to make sure clothes were washed correctly, mended as necessary, ironed, and every piece sorted into the correct student's box.

Vivian also began to teach home economics. One of the projects assigned was a rice pudding. Joyce Baker (now Porte) recalls this day

Herbert with the RVA chorus, circa 1956
Front: Martha Woll, Lila Propst, Lois Hollenbeck, Judy Retherford,
Phyllis Kardatske, Mildred Wolf, Naomi Glock, Ruth Glock
Back: Herbert Downing, Jeanette Krieger, Grace Lyon, Dick Boda,
Jon Moris, Edwin Downing, David Morrow

well, as she had made her rice pudding and put it into the oven at the Hollenbeck's. Since this was the last class of the day and she had a responsibility at the student candy store after school, Mrs. Hollenbeck told her to go ahead to her job, and daughter Lois would remove the pudding when it was done. Unfortunately, both girls forgot the pudding; before they knew it, the kerosene stove had caught the kitchen—and subsequently the whole house—on fire. Herbert had some ammunition stored in the attic that commenced to explode, causing many to think the Mau Mau had attacked. This was 1954, and the school was very aware of the Mau Mau threats. The school was enclosed with barbwire fencing, and older boys and men walked the campus at night to keep watch.

Lila Propst (now Balisky) recalls the day of the Downing house fire as a prayer day. All the missionaries were assembled at the Teasdales' home, which was down at the very lowest place on the station. They had the phone off the hook so they would not be disturbed during prayer. Lila was up at the highest road of the station, in their home called Twin Gables, when suddenly she heard the African distress cry. Thinking it was a Mau Mau raid, she ran for the pistol her parents kept in the cedar chest in their room. Although she tried phoning the adults, as did others down at the fire, there was no response since the phone was off the hook. Going outside, she saw the fire down the hill.

Very little was salvaged from the fire, and all of the precious pictures and items stored in the upstairs were lost. Fortunately there was no loss of life, but the loss of the Downings' and Hollenbecks' possessions was considerable. For several years the empty lot where the house once stood was a grim reminder of that terrible day.

***

Several of the older boys who knew how to use guns were given shifts under the leadership of Welles Devitt to patrol the campus at night. Paul Teasdale (Junky), Paul Skoda (Skipps), Edwin Wines (Tex), and David Kellum (Kelly) were among those given this responsibility. Fortunately they never had to use the guns.

Several events during this terrible time stand out in students' minds as they relate and relive the Mau Mau uprisings. Just up the hill, a few miles from RVA, and on the top of the escarpment, the village called Lari was attacked. The huts were set on fire and people trying to escape hacked to death. During the long night, although the students at RVA could not see Lari, they did see flames and smoke coming from other burning huts on the escarpment south of Kijabe.

In the earlier part of the same evening, a group of 80 Mau Mau had descended on the police station at Naivasha down in the valley, about eighteen miles from Kijabe, stolen submachine guns and ammunition, and freed 173 Mau Mau prisoners before fleeing into the night.

The next day, some Mau Mau were captured near RVA and were being taken to the Kijabe police station. The officer on duty, thinking of the horrible happenings of the night before, opened fire. Before he realized what he had done, two Home Guard men were dead and several injured. It was obvious that nerves were at a breaking point.

On March 28, 1953, an incident occurred that is related at RVA reunions to this day. After the students went to bed, they were awakened by the alarm bell. Immediately alert, they heard shots up the hill and sounds of the campus guards heading up the hill. After a time the "all clear" was sounded and the guards returned.

Less than a month later a band of Mau Mau were captured by the Home Guards, with the assistance of the RVA boys. These men, under questioning, admitted an attempt on the school. The Mau Mau men said that when they had come down to attack the school, they had abandoned the idea because the school was so heavily surrounded by British soldiers all dressed in luminescent white uniforms.

Ironically, in March of 1953 there were no British soldiers at the school. Many believe that God sent angels to protect the children at RVA, surrounding them with His guardian angels in the form of British soldiers.

Those were trying times for RVA, and Herbert Downing. Keeping the school functioning, maintaining the academic program, and meeting the emotional needs of the students was not an easy job. During those days and nights of fear and uncertainty, the students and faculty found their faith to be the main source of solace, maturing them in a way that no school-provided Scripture lessons could have done.

Ruth Ann Downing (now Miano) tells of their gardener at Kijabe who was murdered by the Mau Mau. This left his son David Mwangi an orphan. Herbert Downing unofficially adopted the boy, paying for his school fees and counseling him along the way. He became so much a part of the family that she and brother Martin considered David as their sibling. David eventually qualified to become a clerk and worked in the RVA office. During their return visit to Kenya and RVA in 1981, Herb and Mildred went with Ken and Ivy to visit David, his wife, and their three children.

Jomo Kenyatta, who had been incarcerated in the remote northern frontier of Kenya, came up for trial in April 1953. Worried that this would cause increased tensions, it was decided to cut the school term short so that RVA students would be home with their parents.

It was during this time that, recognizing the vulnerability of the community of Christians at Kijabe, the colonial government had deployed a group of Lancashire Fusiliers to RVA under the leadership of an officer nicknamed "Chips." Needless to say, these happenings affected RVA and the students there, as the men were housed under the front porch of the Kiambogo building. There was fear that the Mau Mau would see the student body as a way to retaliate against the white man and those following their religion. A bell system was used to communicate problems or an "all's well." A seven-foot-high tangle of barbed wire was erected around the campus, and bamboo shoots trimmed into spikes made a secondary fence. Those precautions and the patrolling of the campus gave some sense of security to the frightened children.

Following the release of Kenyatta after his trial, the country was pleasantly surprised that the situation quieted. The British government agreed to give Kenya its independence, and on December 12, 1963, the Union Jack came down and the new Kenya flag was raised. Mr. Kenyatta became the first president of the new republic. Over the next few years, many of the settlers left Kenya, believing they could not live under the new rule, given the changes made in requirements for business and land holdings. Ironically, missionaries found that the new government welcomed their help and appreciated the education and resources provided.

RVA, although it had been growing gradually, now took a growth spurt. By 1958 the student body was close to one hundred. This number continued to climb. As new missionaries came out, more station kids (those living on the station with their parents) were able to walk to school and did not have to occupy dormitory space. But with this growing population came new challenges and problems.

14.

RVA After Independence

Kenya's independence quickly brought the problems of segregation to the fore. No longer could a school be an all-white school. Although RVA's primary purpose was to serve the missions community, they were now required to admit Kenyans. Ten percent was the suggested number.

Herbert knew that Kenyan students must be selected carefully. They would need to know enough English to survive the school environment, they would need to be intellectually capable of competing with missionary kids, and they would need to be able to fit into the living conditions of the boarding school. Finding African students who met the above criteria and whose parents could pay the school fees, although discounted, could be a challenge. Applications flew in by the hundreds.

Herbert approached Ted Honer, who was serving on staff, about this problem and asked that he do the screening of students and to select those he felt confident could be successful at RVA. Choosing the right students was an important task because they must be successful, or RVA might suffer from all sorts of recriminations, thus jeopardizing the cause of missions in East Africa.

Ted accepted the job and began sorting through the applications. Many of the applicants were much too old to fit into the RVA student body. Some knew very little English, and many had little formal education. Interviews had to be set up to determine the English language ability. American standardized tests were given to evaluate the child's competency with academic knowledge. Reading, writing and spelling in English were evaluated, and the level of mathematics skill tested. Eventually the list got whittled down to a very few. These were then presented to Herb Downing and the school board.

Fortunately, those accepted generally fit in well and were successful students, making those in power aware that RVA was indeed a school of which Kenya could be proud. In fact, Vice President Daniel Arap Moi chose to send his sons to RVA. Moi had become a Christian under the tutelage of missionaries and had gone on to work in one of the mission's teacher training schools before getting into government. Both Kenyatta and Moi maintained a friendship with the school and were generally supportive of missions.

***

Unfortunately, the 1950s and '60s found several other African countries in turmoil. Don and Ruth Fonseca were working in the Sudan, but in November 1963 had to evacuate. They chose to go to Congo because that is where their daughter was in school at Rethy Academy. Don began teaching fifth and sixth grades at Rethy. Before long, the unrest in Congo meant that all the missionaries had to once again evacuate. Don and Ruth were due for furlough but got a letter from John Barney at RVA asking them to consider coming to Kenya to teach at RVA. They accepted the invitation and arrived at Kijabe in August of 1964.

Don was a gifted musician whose forte was choral music; he therefore got several choirs going, as well as maintaining the instrumental groups. Herbert Downing was anxious to have a good choir and worked with Don until choral music became a daily class, with enough practice time to put out a quality product. The instrumental music now took a back seat to the choral, although Don was a polished trumpet player and certainly appreciated the instrumental music program. Before long, the RVA choir was being asked to appear for concerts in Nairobi at the National Theatre. It was also

Herbert and Martin Downing join President Jomo Kenyatta for a performance of the RVA chorus

invited to the home of President Jomo Kenyatta, where he listened and obviously thoroughly enjoyed the presentations; he asked them back on several subsequent occasions. The choir made annual concert tours in addition to performing on campus. Many of the choir members were also athletes, and some found themselves doing double duty as, for example, on the annual rugby and choir tour to Arusha, Tanzania.

Don tells of one time when the group had performed for the president. They were sitting in the backyard of his home talking and enjoying refreshments, when the president begged his pardon saying, "I must talk with this man." With that he turned to Herbert Downing. Soon they were off, conversing in Kikuyu. After a while, Kenyatta turned to Don and said, "This man speaks like one of us. In fact, his Kikuyu is probably better than mine."

Don and Ruth finally went on their furlough in 1967, returning the next year to resume the music program at RVA. They ultimately gave RVA eleven years. When they returned to the States, Don took a position at Stoneybrook High School on Long Island, where he worked for another seven years.

***

Paul Lyons and his brother Steven were part of a large group of students who were evacuated from Congo and enrolled at RVA. They were not AIM children, but Paul immediately noticed that their denominational affiliation was inconsequential to both staff and students. Everyone was an RVAite. Paul became a player on the first rugby team at RVA and learned that one of the sports traditions was to treat the visiting team to tea. He was very impressed with the Downings' willingness to open their home to thirty-five or more sweaty rugby players.

David Lyons, another brother, came to Kenya after his college graduation from Westmont College en route to Congo to see his parents. In Nairobi, he made a wrong turn on a borrowed motorcycle and was killed by an oncoming car. This was a terrible blow to his family and the whole RVA community. Paul recalls the Herbert Downings opening their home to the family and friends who came for the funeral. It was Kenneth Downing, living in Nairobi at that time, who called Paul in California to tell him of his brother's death. Ken and Ivy made sure that details were taken care of, family members contacted, and funeral arrangements made at Kijabe. Between the two Downing families, they made sure that the Lyons family was all right.

***

With RVA getting more and more students, the dormitories became overcrowded, and finding spaces for those students it was obliged to serve became a major problem for Herb. Turning to the other missions who sent their children to RVA, he asked their pleasure. Would they rather start their own school, or would they prefer to give RVA a surcharge in order that RVA could build more space? Money appeared to be much the better option, and the missions contributing students began contributing money for building.

A new dormitory necessitated more classroom space. That necessitated dining room space. That necessitated a new kitchen, and on and on. Herbert found himself doing planning, preparing drawings, supervising building, and attending to many other varied and sundry tasks, along with running a school. It seemed there was one *shauri* after the other.

During this period, the Herb Downings worked in one more brief furlough. On March 1 of 1965, they flew home via Hawaii. After only a six-month leave, they returned that same year on September 21, shortly after the beginning of the school term. Mildred resumed teaching immediately, and Herb was deep into the running of the school before his feet had hardly had time to touch ground. Being completely fluent in Kikuyu was both a blessing and at times a curse. Every African who came by wanted to talk with *Bwana Herberti*. Missionaries needed someone to act as liaison for one of their *shauris*. A teacher was having a problem with a student or some other concern. There were trips to town for supplies and problems at the building sites. Herbert Downing was patience itself with all these interruptions and diverse problems.

***

One habit or ritual that perhaps saved him was afternoon tea served at the Downing house each afternoon at 4:00 p.m., without fail. Mildred was sure to get home in time to have the water boiled and some goodies ready. Sometimes it was only her own family who would be there, but at other times guests stopped by. She was always the gracious hostess and welcomed any who came.

Daughter Gayle wrote in her memoirs that Mildred, soon after coming to Kenya, set this time aside for family in the event they needed something. The children would always know Mom could be found at home at four o'clock every day. Gayle related the experience of receiving a note one day from her mother stating that some government officials would be at the house that afternoon for tea. Mildred was her teacher, so dismissed Gayle to go home to prepare tea and to welcome the guests. Getting home, Gayle discovered no cookies, cakes, or anything else to serve with tea. Her sixth grade brother, Eddie Lee, happened to be home, so the two got busy and made a batch of scones, or biscuits. One third were baked plain, to another third they added cheese, and to the last batch they added raisins. Fortunately the biscuits turned out well.

By the time the guests arrived, the table was set, the tea was made, and the hot biscuits were ready to eat. Both parents appreciated the efforts of their children and applauded them; the children learned how to pitch in and how to work together in a pinch. On another occasion, when Herb had traveled to Congo with Gayle and Glenn, leaving Ruth Ann and Eddie Lee home, some very wealthy guests arrived just at teatime. Undaunted, Ruth Ann and Eddie Lee got busy and produced a plate of tomato and lettuce sandwiches and also poured tea for the guests. The guests were impressed and chose to return for a subsequent visit to the home "where the children were so well trained that they could take over adult tasks."

Mildred was widely noted for her gracious hospitality. Her table was always well set, her house clean and tidy, and the food exceptional. No matter the time of day or weather condition, Mildred always looked like she had just dressed and combed her hair. Neatness and grace were certainly two of her many virtues. Being invited for a meal at the Downing home was considered a treat.

Mildred was also an excellent teacher and took on several varied assignments during her time at RVA. Eleanor Morrison (now Kennedy) says that Ma Herb was her absolutely favorite math teacher, which

Mildred, ever the gracious hostess, and Herbert (with his back to the camera). On his left, Judy Cooke, Verity Coder, Ina Reed, Mildred, Clara Barrett, Faye Leitch, Martin.

is probably why she became an accountant. Mildred was also a good Sunday School teacher. Eleanor recalled Mildred's challenge to maintain high moral standards as young women. She challenged the girls to save themselves for the man they would marry. Eleanor vowed that she would strive to save herself. Mildred challenged her class, "If you do, mark my words, you'll remember this class when you walk down the aisle on your wedding day." Eleanor did, and quietly thanked God on the way down the aisle for Mrs. Downing's inspirational lessons. Eleanor and her husband Ted have been married for nearly fifty years and say that, given the choice, they would do it all over the same way.

Lila Propst (now Balisky) also appreciated Mildred's Bible lessons. She especially recalls going through *Highlights of Scripture* by Henrietta Mears. During Lila's senior year, Mildred became ill for several months and asked Lila if she would be willing to teach her French class for her. Lila loved teaching the grammar, but discovered that she was not a conversationalist. As a thank you, Mildred gave Lila a Thompson Chain-Reference Bible that she has to this day. In it Mildred wrote:

To Lila W. Propst
In appreciation for your help with the French class when I was
incapacitated.
Given—July 24ᵗʰ, 1958
Best Wishes for the future—
Lotsalove
Mildred H. Downing

That inscription is still very special to Lila.

***

Not all the "saints" were so saintly though. Eleanor Morrison (now Kennedy) told about the day Harold LaFont (now Dr. LaFont, physician) put a tiny mouse under the bell that stood on Mrs. Downing's desk. Eleanor commented, "It's a good job Harold was one of Ma Herb's favorites!"

It was not only Mildred who held the respect of the students, but Herbert also shared admiration. Ann Propst (now Pallex), who lived at Kijabe right next door to the Downings, was home reading and became so engrossed in her story that, when she finally came to, she found the house strangely quiet. She started walking through the house and couldn't locate her sister or mother or any of the African help. Looking out, she could not see anyone at her grandmother's house either. Just about the time she was beginning to panic, and wondering if the rapture had happened and she was left behind, she saw Mr. Downing in his yard next door. What a great relief that was! She knew that Herb Downing was much too good to be left behind.

Ann also remembers the night her family was taking a plane from Nairobi to return to the United States. As often happened during those days, when they got to the airport, they found that the plane's departure was delayed until the next day. Back they came to Kijabe, where Mildred put them up for the night so they could make the trip into Nairobi again the next day.

Henrietta Propst, known to the students as Ma Henny or Ma Propst, was an excellent teacher and seldom had any problems in her classes. However, one little boy was having a hard time controlling

113

himself, and in desperation Henrietta took him down to the principal's office for a caning. Caning was a standard type of discipline in those early days, and Herbert Downing kept several canes for unruly kids. The boy was duly caned, and as the chastised student and Henrietta walked back up the hill he kept repeating, "Mrs. Propst, I really needed that." Maintaining a well-disciplined student body was important to Herbert Downing. He followed up on reported infractions and yet always studied the situation and tried to fit the punishment to the infraction.

John Skoda recalls that Herb was very good about writing letters of recommendation for the students who were leaving and on their way to colleges and universities. Mildred was also good about wishing students well as they moved on into "life after RVA."

John also relates an incident that meant a lot to him as a little boy and that illustrates the caring the two Downing families had for the students at RVA. He had been hospitalized with glandular fever at Gertrude's Garden, a children's hospital in Nairobi. He felt very lonely and isolated, as his parents were far away in Ogada, which is up closer to Lake Victoria, so he truly appreciated visits by Ivy Downing during that time. Upon his release from the hospital, the Herbert Downings made arrangements for him to stay with Jim and Trixie Hodson at the Red Earth Farm in Limuru, where he could recover and gain his strength before coming back to school. Jim Hodson was a former RVA student and had remained good friends with Herb and Mildred Downing. Jim and Trixie often came to Kijabe for church on Sunday and remained avid supporters of RVA, allowing picnics and student visits to their farm. In 1975, John was able to take his children to the Red Earth Farm to thank the Hodsons for their caring and generosity.

Lanny Arensen recalls Mildred as his Latin teacher. At this point he recalls "hic, haec, hoc," but that is about all. He does not remember that class as being much of a fun experience for him, but he does have high praise for the teacher who did her best to pull him through.

He remembers Herbert Downing as the principal and felt fortunate that he did not have the occasion to go visit him at his office. He does recall one chapel message from Psalm 118:24, "This is the day the Lord has made: Let us be glad and rejoice in it." That message for some reason made a profound impression and has stuck with Lanny.

Lanny also recalls the day Herbert Downing made an apology to the school. Earlier in the school term he told the whole school that someone had scratched his new Volkswagen with a nail, writing the name Downing onto the door or fender. He wanted the culprit to come forward and confess, as he was sure it was one of the students. For a while the students looked at each other, and everyone felt a sense of guilt. Now he stood in front of the assembled student body and relayed that the culprit had been found. The guilty party was none other than his own son Martin, and he apologized for accusing the students. Lanny appreciated the humility and honesty displayed.

Chris Nelson, who was a gifted pianist, recalls the Downings driving him to Nairobi in their family car when he was involved in the Kenya Music Festival. He recalls they were the sponsors for the class of 1961 and accompanied the senior class on their safari to Mombasa. He was impressed with Herbert's ability to pitch a tent and set up camp without a great show, even making the process look simple. Chris had come to RVA in 1957 from Tanzania. His father worked for the Meru tribe on Mt. Meru near Arusha.

The Nelsons were not missionaries, but RVA arranged for Chris and his sister to attend RVA between 1957 and 1964. During Chris's senior year, Mr. Nelson had political problems with the Kenya government administration, and he was prohibited from entering Kenya. Because the children were already enrolled at RVA—Chris in his last year, and both children doing very well with their studies—the Nelsons decided to send the children anyway. The president of the Meru-Co-op, Sangito Lucas, who was a very tall and good-natured African coffee farmer, thought it a privilege to be the one to drive the Nelson children to school. When they arrived at RVA, the Downings were personally concerned for the welfare of the children and their driver, and put the driver up in their house overnight. It was those kinds of incidents that put Herbert and Mildred high on the respect list.

Herbert had never forgotten the fact that AIM was in Africa to serve the Africans. The Rift Valley Academy's purpose was to assist in this cause by caring for and educating the children of those missionaries. With this thought in mind, he worked closely with the African leaders in the community and also with the many workmen that the school employed. Herb wanted to make sure that his men learned good business principles, and he helped them begin savings accounts. Each pay period he would help them deposit a little toward their savings account. Soon some of the vegetable ladies who came around to the homes selling their garden produce asked Herbert if he could do the same for them. His rapport and standing with the local people was great. His knowing Kikuyu and having grown up among them was a major factor in their great trust in him.

Mid-term at school meant another time when students could go home or be joined with their families. However, for some the distances were too far either for the parents to come to Kenya for a long weekend or for the children to get home and back. It was on one of these mid-term breaks that the Herbert Downings and one of the African *mzee*s (wise old man) took a few of the older boys for a never-to-be-forgotten hike into the forests surrounding the school.

***

Another major happening in the early '60s was the introduction of basketball and then rugby. Mr. Lehrer, during his time as homemaker, had taught the older students the game of softball. There was a nice field leveled that did well as a softball field. When Ted Honer arrived in 1958, he began teaching physical education and started a basketball team. One of the first school holidays was spent making a basketball court right in front of the school where a tennis court used to be. Basketball had become popular in Nairobi among British servicemen, and some of the African schools also had teams.

Herbert takes a group of students on a hike.
Here he stops to talk with an *mzee*.
Photo provided by Chris Nelson

Soon RVA was competing with men and boys from Nairobi and surrounding schools.

The "Cameronians," a squadron of British military men, were generally much older than the seventeen and eighteen year old RVA students, but RVA boys had some major advantages. Kijabe is situated at 7,600 feet in altitude. These boys had good lungs. They also did not smoke. The poor "old men" would huff and pant while RVA kids ran them to death up and down the court. Needless to say, what the boys lacked in height and experience was more than made up in lung power and stamina.

Dave Reynolds started the boys playing rugby or British football. Since Kenya was a former British colony, this was a well-known game and was already popular in local schools. It did not take long before RVA was competing with the best teams in the country. In subsequent years RVA frequently took the trophy for best team.

During a long furlough, Ted Honer worked on a master's degree and made a plan for a gymnasium at RVA as his project. Several years later his nephew, Willard Andersen, erected a gym using many of the ideas from Ted's original thesis. That gym is well used to this day.

All these innovations had to be run past Herbert Downing, and most also required school board approval. One of the things that most staff members appreciated about Herbert Downing was his ability to flex and a willingness to listen. One never got the impression that he was quick with a negative before giving the request or idea his thoughtful consideration. Usually when he said "no" there was good reason.

Howard Andersen told about his experience when asked to restructure the multipurpose building called Jubilee Hall. He presented his ideas to Herbert, who agreed with his plan. The problem came with the workmen who did not want to do the work the way it was designed. After a few words from *Bwana Herberti* the building proceeded as planned. When working with both Africans and missionaries, Herbert commanded respect.

***

With RVA getting larger, and since it now had a full high school, the idea of accreditation seemed like a next step. Having just served on several accreditation committees in the Western Association of Schools and Colleges, Ted Honer suggested that accreditation be considered. Herbert Downing was all for the idea and set Ted to work. Since RVA serves children from all across the United States, application was made to the Middle States Association. The association replied, and soon an initial team of educators that they sent from Nairobi arrived at RVA and gave their recommendation to proceed with the accreditation process. Soon after this, the Honers left for the States, and Roy Entwistle was left with the huge task of getting everything ready for the review process. After Roy coordinated the writing of curricula, preparation of plans, and filling out of reports by the hundreds, a team from the United States finally arrived to investigate this application. On June 4, 1968, RVA received notice from the Middle States Association of Colleges and Schools that accreditation had been granted for a three-year period ending December 31, 1971.

Suggestions for improvement were made, but since at that time initial accreditation was never given for more than three years, this was a wonderful boost. (Currently, accreditation may be given for ten years, with a review at five years.) So many RVA students continue on to major colleges and universities that accreditation is essential for them to gain entrance. Since this initial acceptance, RVA has continued in good standing and has maintained the high standards necessary for ongoing accreditation.

RVA now had a completely separate elementary school with its classrooms and dorms on an upper campus. The children still shared dining room and laundry facilities, but in general the elementary school was apart from the upper grades. With his mounting responsibilities, Herbert Downing suggested appointing a principal for the elementary school. It had operated with a head teacher for some time, but now Roy Entwistle was selected as principal. The elementary school was usually about a fourth of the total student body.

Another major change affecting the student body was the number of missionaries living at Kijabe, as that number had also multiplied, making many more pupils day students. These students, because they were able to walk to school each day, did not require dormitory space but did need classroom space.

The school had grown and grown. Finally the school board determined that a cap must be put on the number that RVA could handle; they chose five hundred as the top limit. On a few occasions, that limit was broken, but it remained the suggested ceiling.

Kenneth and Ivy Downing

15.

Ken and Ivy Back at Nyakach

When Ken and Ivy stepped in for a year as RVA homemakers in 1953, they continued their work at Nyakach during school breaks. At this time, Ken was appointed acting field director for AIM. After they moved back to Nyakach in June of 1955, Ken was then made general field secretary of the International Conference, which was the highest office of AIM on the field.

This came right at a time when family life was ramping up. In August, Daphne graduated from RVA and the Ken Downing family left Kenya for a furlough. Gone were the days of slow boat travel. This time they flew via England where they were able to visit with Ivy's aunt Phyllis. The family then headed for Canada, where Daphne enrolled for grade thirteen in Hamilton, Ontario. The next year she went to Barrington Bible College in Providence, Rhode Island. After two years she enrolled at West Suburban Hospital School of Nursing in Oak Park, Illinois.

In October of 1956, Ken and Ivy with their four younger children returned to Kenya to resume their work at Nyakach. When David graduated from RVA in 1958, he traveled home to the United States with Herbert and Muriel Cook and their son Ron; there he enrolled at Moody Bible Institute in Chicago.

When Dottie graduated from RVA in 1961, she chose to attend Freeman Business College in Oak Park, Illinois. That same year, Daphne received her RN from West Suburban Hospital School of Nursing, giving reason for the whole family to come home to the United States for their year of furlough. This time they stayed in Oak Park, Illinois, so that they could all be together.

The following year, in September 1962, Ivy and the two younger boys, Lee and Vic, returned to Kenya while Ken used the opportunity to visit several West African countries. When he arrived back in October, Ken and Ivy moved from Nyakach to Nairobi to start working with the Association of Evangelicals of Africa and Madagascar (AEAM). This new assignment placed Ken in a position to observe the work of missions in many of the sub-Saharan countries of Africa, and it required lots of travel.

In 1964, Ken's sister Lucile and her husband, Bob Sawhill, decided to visit Kenya. This was the first time Lucile had been back since going home to the US to finish school in 1920, so she was excited to return to her roots and to show off her heritage to husband Bob. She found many changes at Kijabe and RVA but enjoyed showing her husband the old homestead and where she had gone to school. Ken and Ivy took them into Uganda and Congo, giving Lucile and Bob the opportunity to experience a large part of Africa on their trip.

The next few years saw Lee graduating from RVA and enrolling at Columbia Bible College, South Carolina, in 1967. Vic graduated in 1968 from RVA and went to Taylor University in Upland, Indiana. David got married, and he and his wife, Diane, went to Congo as missionaries in 1960. Daughter Daphne married Gordon McRostie in 1965 and went to serve in Morocco.

Many years later at a reunion of the party of new missionaries with whom Ivy had sailed from New York, Lucilda Newton, who was one of them, asked Ivy about her grown children. Ivy began by telling her that Daphne, her eldest, was married to Gordon McRostie, a missionary kid who grew up in Mali, West Africa. She added that they were currently serving the Lord in Morocco, North Africa.

"McRostie!" Lucilda exclaimed, "Do you remember when the time came in New York for our ship to leave for Kenya, we had a farewell dinner at AIM headquarters? I invited friends from my home church in Duluth, Minnesota, who were also in New York waiting for their ship to sail, returning to West Africa for their second term of missionary service. You held their little six-month-old baby that evening. That little fellow was Gordon McRostie, son of Loyd and Marjorie McRostie of Gospel Missionary Union!"

***

Ken resigned his affiliation with the AEAM in January 1971. He and Ivy moved to Nakuru, where he was to do Africa Inland Church work and also to organize AIM archives. By now their children were scattered all over the world; Daphne in Morocco; David in Congo; Dottie, who worked in Nairobi, was in the United States for a short furlough; Lee in Viet Nam serving Uncle Sam; and Vic at Ball State University doing pre-med studies.

Once again, Ken's linguistic ability was a definite asset with the work at Nakuru. Besides his Kikuyu, he was now fluent in Swahili and had gained a working knowledge of Luo, although he was reluctant to speak that language. When the Africa Inland Church was revising its constitution, which had been written in both English and Kiswahili in 1972, Ken was asked to proofread the Swahili version to be sure it was grammatically correct and an exact translation of the English.

Christmas of 1972 brought Herbert and Mildred, Ruth Ann and a girlfriend Judy Ouland, and old friends Claudon and Gladys Stauffacher to Nakuru to celebrate Christmas with Ken and Ivy. Although their own children were in the far-flung reaches of the earth, it was good to have family and friends with whom to celebrate Christ's birth.

In May 1973, Ken and Ivy moved back to Nyakach. Ken's work at Nyakach was primarily church work that required sitting in *barazas* (council meetings) and attending meetings conducted in Luo. He learned how to hear the language, but being a perfectionist, never felt he had the correct pronunciation or fluency for speech. For speaking he reverted to Kiswahili, which was the trade language understood by most Africans. The following year they took a short furlough to visit Daphne and Gordon in Rabat, Morocco. They then attended Vic's graduation from Taylor University on May 19, and then his wedding to Lynda Myers on June 8.

In 1976, Ken was diagnosed by Dr. David Silverstein in Nairobi with a heart valve problem. By January 1977 it became necessary to replace the valve, so he went to Chicago for the surgery. Eight months later, in Evanston, Illinois, while having dinner with Gordon and Daphne, Ken suffered cardiac arrest. But apparently he made a satisfactory recovery, enabling his return to Kenya. He continued on as though nothing had happened but faithfully had check-ups with Dr. Silverstein in Nairobi and actually appeared to be in general good health.

During the next few years Ken and Ivy continued to work at Nyakach and enjoyed visits from their children and guests as they came through. Their family was expanding, as each of their five children were now married and having children of their own.

***

By 1980 the Ken Downings were slowing down a bit. They were both in their seventies, and Ken had already had a valve replacement, which meant he could not do as much as he had done in his youth.

In 1981, RVA celebrated its seventy-fifth anniversary. Herbert and Mildred were able to return to Kenya to join Ken and Ivy for this celebration. For both brothers it was a time of bittersweet and kaleidoscopic memories as they recalled their time as students, teachers, homemakers, and administrators. Almost any job that needed doing at RVA had been done by Downings, even that of the kitchen and laundry supervision.

Back at home in Nyakach, the typical day began with Ken fixing and bringing Ivy a cup of tea, which she drank while dressing. Then there was the daily radio call, followed by breakfast. Ken was known for his love of tea, and if offered water he would retort with "more people drown in water than in tea." Perhaps the habit came as a result of his many visits to African homes. Rather than chance drinking water that was not safe, he always suggested a cup of *chai* (tea boiled with milk and sugar) that required the water as well as the milk be boiled. This precaution prevented dysentery, which is a constant plague for missionaries.

The daily routine sometimes included a drive to Kisumu for groceries and supplies. Other times Ken drove about eight miles to Sondu to pick up the mail. But the day never started without devotions after breakfast, consisting of a reading from *Daily Light* that would be followed by prayer. This always included all the children and any other family members who came to mind. The daily suggestions for prayer made in the *Fuel For Prayer Fires*, a publication of AIM, were included along with local work and workers.

Tea was once again served at 11:00 a.m. on the screen porch overlooking the Sondu Valley and Lake Victoria. This break was brief and work quickly resumed. Lunch was at 1:00 p.m., after which a short nap prepared them for the work of the afternoon. Ken often had paperwork in his office, as he took care of all the church council finances. With retirement looming he had tried to train Africans to take over the District Church Council accounts, and he finally found a man whom he could trust and who learned the necessary accounting skills.

Christmas time at Nyakach meant a different sort of celebration. Churches from about a fifteen-mile radius would come to a large local gathering held under the jacaranda trees on the side of the Downing home. Here different choirs and groups gave presentations that lasted hour upon hour. Then came the gathering of the gifts. The local churches broke up into their respective groups and took an annual offering. As they came together, the roll was called and an accounting made. If the sum exceeded the previous year, a great shout of celebration was heard. If the offering was not as good, the churches were asked to try again. When the final tally was acceptable, the whole congregation rejoiced. From this sum and the weekly offerings, the pastors would be paid throughout the year. Ken was responsible for banking or storing the monies and seeing they were dispersed appropriately.

Ivy topped off Christmas Day with an especially good dinner, and a good time was had by all.

By November of 1981, Ivy, who had been experiencing severe pain, had her gall bladder removed. At that time it was discovered that she had an enlarged liver, but she was assured there was no malignancy.

Again in 1983, Ivy was seeing doctors for persistent pain attributed to the enlarged liver. The diagnosis was: "Definitely no malignancy. Most probably primary biliary cirrhosis of the liver." For a time Ivy appeared to be doing better, although some of her discomfort persisted.

At the urging of their family, Ken and Ivy took a five-month furlough, April to August 1983. It proved to be a very special time that included many eventful family occasions: during a stopover in Morocco, they witnessed their two grandchildren Cyndi and Kenny McRostie, baptized in the Atlantic Ocean; in Teaneck, New Jersey, they attended son Vic's ordination in the Evangelical Free Church; they had time with Herb, Mildred, and Lucile—the first in nineteen years; and the second week of August found all their children and grandchildren together for a reunion in Teaneck (twelve adults and fourteen grandchildren). With four families in missions, that was quite a feat! Ken and Ivy and the Hildebrandts left a few days later to return to Kenya.

Recognizing that Ken and Ivy were not as well as they once were and really needed help, the mission sent Chuck and Bobbie Kinzer to Nyakach for about nine months. During 1985, Don and Leslie Walcott moved to Nyakach, and Betty Thompson, a nurse, was sent there for one year. Scott and Barbara Harbert went to Nyakach later. In some ways the additional help was a blessing; in others it created more work because Ken and Ivy had to assist the newer folk with adjustments, language, and adapting to the new region.

On September 9, 1986, Ivy fell on the kitchen floor in their home at Nyakach, breaking her right hip. The break required surgery, and she was forbidden to put weight on the leg for six months. This made it impossible for Ivy to maintain a home and take care of the daily necessities of life. It was decided that they should move Ivy to Eldoret to stay with Dottie, and Ken would commute back and forth to Nyakach, where he was managing the finances for the work. The six-month stay with Dottie stretched to one year before Ivy was able to return to Nyakach.

On December 15, 1986, Ken and Ivy heard the sad news that Herbert had died in Illinois.

The year 1987 brought Ken and Ivy's fiftieth wedding anniversary, and all the children, with several of the grandchildren, went to Kenya for the celebration. Ken also had hip replacement surgery in Nairobi, and Ivy had the plate removed from her hip. During this time away from Nyakach, Ken had been asked to sort through the AIM Kenya archives for the microfilming of important documents and information to be stored at the Billy Graham Center in Wheaton, Illinois.

Early 1988 found Ken and Ivy well enough to be back at Nyakach. Ken was still the Lake District regional treasurer and also the District Council treasurer. This meant he had to attend meetings of the Central Church Council in March, which required driving down-country over less-than-wonderful roads.

During the Kenya Field Conference held at Kijabe in December, Ken and Ivy were recognized for fifty-five years of service with

Africa Inland Mission. It had been a long time since Ken and Ivy met and fell in love so many years ago.

On January 4, 1989, Ken had severe pain around his sternum region that lasted all afternoon and throughout the night. Dottie went to Nyabondo near Sondu where she hoped to get some advice from the doctor at the Catholic mission. She had tried to reach Dr. Silverstein in Nairobi to no avail. It was decided that despite the fact that it was four in the afternoon, the best thing was to head to Nairobi for medical help. After they stopped twice before Kericho so that Ken could relieve himself, the lights on the car went out at the bottom of the Mau escarpment. Even though in pain, Ken managed to get the lights working again by using aluminum foil in the fuse. Once they reached Nakuru, they called ahead to alert Deb Richards at Kenya Branch, the AIM office in Nairobi, that they were on the way. Between Nakuru and Nairobi they encountered heavy rain, making the roads horrible and conditions hazardous. Deb Richards had been trying to call Dr. Silverstein all evening but still had not reached him by the time the Downings arrived. She put Ken, Ivy, and Dottie up in a friend's house for the night.

The next day they were able to get through to Dr. Silverstein's office and went to it, hoping to be fitted in. Both Ken and Ivy were in wheelchairs, with Ken holding a basin in case of vomiting. When they finally saw Dr. Silverstein, he admitted Ken to the hospital at about 1:00 p.m. with probable "gastric enteritis." By 5:30 blood was found in the stools and the diagnosis was changed to "erosive gastritis." Several people stepped forward to donate blood. By 9:30 p.m., Ken was moved to the ICU after another big bleeding incident.

In the morning of January 7, after he received two pints of blood, Ken's bleeding seemed to have lessened. He ate a few bites of lunch that Dottie fed to him.

January 8, 1989, while Dottie and Ivy were preparing to go to the hospital, the doctor called to say that Ken had gone. Dottie immediately called her siblings and alerted friends at Nyakach and Kijabe to prepare for a funeral.

The funeral was held at Kijabe on January 14, in the old cemetery down at the bottom of the mission property where so many missionaries have been laid to rest. Ken was buried beside his parents. All five of his children were able to make it to the funeral.

After the funeral, the whole family went to Nyakach, where Ivy valiantly accepted the condolences of the local people who came by to see her. The family helped empty the house and, over the next five weeks, moved Ivy to Dottie and Jonathan's home in Eldoret.

In April, Ivy complained of a sore, red ankle and calf, so Dottie took her to see one of the AIM doctors, Dr. Ann Peterson, who consulted with Dr. Silverstein. At their advice Dottie and Ivy left immediately for Nairobi, arriving there at 5:15 p.m. Ivy was admitted into the Nairobi Hospital. The next day the swelling and redness were gone, and the doctor was pleased. With this good news Dottie returned to Eldoret so she could pack up her boys, who needed to get to RVA for the start of the school term. On Monday, April 24, she drove the boys to school and kept a 4:00 p.m. dental appointment at Kijabe. While at the dentist's office, she got a call saying that her mother was in cardiac arrest. Dottie left immediately with Sylvia Pollard and went directly to the hospital, only to find that Ivy had died about 4:10 p.m.

On April 29, 1989, Ivy was buried next to her husband at the Kijabe cemetery.

16.

Herbert and Mildred in Retirement

By the early 1970s, attitudes from the sixties in the USA had begun to infiltrate RVA. Although it was not Haight-Ashbury, many of the fashions and behaviors had seeped onto the mission field, and from there to the students. Girls began to arrive at RVA in short skirts and boys with long hair. During the era of uniforms, there was some control of how the students dressed. Having done away with uniforms in the early '70s, it was difficult to tell a student who came from home that her skirt was too short when Mom had given her blessing. Boys with long hair and Mohawks or other unusual styles resented the school telling them it was inappropriate, when parents had sent them off to school looking that way.

The clothing and hair was only part of the problem. Some of the students came with the habit of smoking, drinking, and using drugs. RVA had a no-tolerance rule, so drug usage meant mandatory suspension or even expulsion. Students came from US schools where open expressions of affection between boys and girls were tolerated, but even handholding had always been taboo at RVA. The music some of the newer students arrived with was unacceptable to the school and the older generation.

To add to this mix of problems was the fact that the school population had mushroomed. The dormitories were full to running over, and the staff was stretched to their limit. Many of the new staff had come directly from teaching at American public schools and arrived with the idea they were coming to another American school. They, too, chafed at the restrictions and rules. Many were coming for a short-term assignment of just a year or two, without having a long-term affiliation or loyalty to AIM and its policies. Some failed to understand that the primary purpose of RVA was to keep the missionaries on the field by taking care of the education of the children.

The age-old differences between mission groups began to surface as some organizations were much more liberal than Africa Inland Mission. For some, drinking and smoking were not considered wrong. Others considered AIM and RVA much too rigid and conservative on issues dealing with dress codes and boy-girl relationships and music.

Unfortunately there were some on staff who exacerbated the issues by aiding and abetting the recalcitrant students. Attempts to discipline and advise were thwarted.

Herbert Downing

Herbert Downing found himself in an untenable situation. He could not please the students and their parents and still maintain law and order. On the other side was the school board and the Africa Inland Mission pulling from a much more conservative stance. Dormitory supervisors were dealing with well over fifty students each, and found they could not monitor those who chose to sneak out after lights-out or when no one was around.

Herbert and Mildred had been on the field since 1933 and had seen many changes at RVA and in Africa Inland Mission, as well as in the country of Kenya. They began to realize that it was about time to consider retirement. Their plan was to officially retire in 1975.

Unfortunately, a year before they had planned to announce their retirement, the school board decided to request that they leave RVA as some felt that the job had become too big and too demanding for Herbert. That same year some of the other staff members either resigned or were asked to leave. The very conservative element among missionaries decided that Herbert had lost control and a stronger and firmer hand was necessary. Paul Beverly from

Mildred Downing

Tanzania was selected to replace him, and Roy Entwistle was asked to serve as Beverly's assistant. Herbert had been grooming Roy to take over the position of principal for some time, as Roy had been his assistant principal.

It was not long before it was evident that Paul Beverly did not have the educational background or experience to run a huge operation like RVA. At the end of one year, the reins were turned over to Roy Entwistle. Slowly Roy managed to get control of the situation and righted the school. It required making the number of students per dorm supervisor lower and establishing firmer guidelines for parents and students before accepting students into RVA. Additional staff was added to help with the governance and supervision.

After serving for well over thirty years as principal at RVA and seeing it grow and develop, it was a painful time for Herb and Mildred. However they managed to leave with dignity and grace and packed up for the journey back to life in the United States. They left RVA in September 1974 and moved to Sandwich, Illinois, where they quickly found another field of service with Christian Camping International. Once again Herb's numerous skills were put to good use. They were offered positions working at a camp nearby in Somonauk, Illinois. This camp was located on land that had been donated by someone who knew Edwin Houk, Mildred's brother. Edwin and Ed Ouland, who was the director of the camp, were good friends, so he knew of the skills of Herbert and Mildred and was happy to use their talents for the work of the camp. Herbert fit right into the general maintenance of the place and was especially useful in the old printing shop. He knew how to set type on the old typesetting press, as that was the kind used at Kijabe where Kenneth had worked.

Mildred was in charge of filing, keeping the addresses updated, and mailing. By the time they finally decided it was time to retire, Herbert was eighty and Mildred seventy-eight. Herbert and Mildred continued to live in Sandwich, and were very active in the Somonauk United Presbyterian Church. Herbert sang in the choir, and Mildred helped out using her hospitality skills. They were well loved and appreciated in that church and community.

On June 19, 1981, Herbert and Mildred celebrated their fiftieth wedding anniversary with all their children attending. It was held at Kelley Hall, Muskingum College, New Concord, Ohio. This was where Herb and Mildred originally met, and having the well-attended celebration there was fitting.

Later in 1981 the Downings were asked to return to Kenya for the celebration of the seventy-fifth anniversary of RVA as guests of the school. This invitation did much to help heal some of the wounds felt by not only the Downings, but also so many others who had been affected by the unfortunate circumstances surrounding their leaving.

Mildred wrote the following about the occasion:

Shortly after this big event (50th Anniversary) we took our trip to Kenya to attend as guests at THE SEVENTY-FIFTH ANNIVERSARY OF RIFT VALLEY ACADEMY where we began our mission work in 1933. From a school of less than 40, it has become a first class, American-type boarding school of 440—grades 1–12. We were encouraged to see the improvements in the grounds and buildings and appreciated being honored guests. His Excellency Daniel Arap Moi, President of Kenya, initiated the week of celebrations on July 12th with the following remarks: "What has been done in the complex is unbelievable. Jesus said 'Without Me you can do nothing.' However mighty we are physically, it is only when we depend and submit to Christ that He will be able to assist in whatever we do." President Moi asked for prayer as he is chairman of the OAU (Organization of African Unity) during the next 12 months.

The International Secretary of the Africa Inland Mission had this to say about us: "We were reminded that during this (Herbert's) three decades as RVA Principal, they had laid the base to the solidly Christian institute which RVA has become." We were happy to see RVA's growth under Roy Entwistle's leadership and that of his staff. We enjoyed visiting with "old" and new friends, being entertained in many of their homes, and in the homes of African friends. It was a blessing to see Herbert and Kenneth serving communion along with African Elders in the African Church."

After the festivities at RVA, Herb and Mildred went with Ken and Ivy to Nairobi, where they noticed many changes. The bustling city of Nairobi as it had been during the colonial era had gradually changed to a city of heavy traffic, street hawkers, and diesel air pollution. They then went to Nyakach, where Ken and Ivy were working.

For their Kenya stay, which was a little over a month, Herb and Mildred were given a small duplex at Kijabe that was furnished and stocked with food. One African friend brought a live rooster. David Mwangi, their "African son," brought milk and had them over for a meal. Many of the families at Kijabe had them over for meals, making it a good time for visiting and reminiscing.

The day after they arrived at Kijabe, a former student who was now serving on the RVA staff brought the Downings some cake squares with the following note: "Dear God, I thank you so much the Downings are here! Help that their time here will be special, worthwhile, and beati-full...." Mildred said the trip was all of that and more. She repeated the verse used on the programs for the seventy-fifth anniversary: "Let the name of the Lord be praised."

The celebrations and the honors bestowed on Herb and Mildred at this seventy-fifth anniversary did much to help them realize how much their contribution had meant to so many through the years and how so many staff and students alike would be in heaven to affirm the greeting, "Well done, thou good and faithful servants."

A few years later, back in the States, it was discovered that Herbert had prostate cancer that had metastasized, leaving him ill and in constant pain. He battled this for six months before he found release in death. After he had been in the hospital a while, it was decided that he should spend his remaining days in the care of his physician son, Ed, in Oshkosh, Wisconsin. He was transported by ambulance to Oshkosh, where he lived until December 15, 1986. He had celebrated his eighty-first birthday on August 14 that year. Mildred, their five children, brother Kenneth, sister Lucile, and eleven grandchildren and two great-grandchildren survived him.

The following thoughts expressed at his funeral by his daughter Ruth Ann Miano lend an insight into the man as his children knew him. They are addressed to the Lord.

Letter of Recommendation

It has been my pleasure to have Herbert C. Downing as father and friend for the past 44 years. He had graduated from this life

Summa Cum Laude, and will be furthering his education in the knowledge of God. He will now have the advantage of sitting at the feet of God himself, and of learning from Him face to face. God will explain to him, lovingly, all the mysteries and dilemmas that puzzled him while he walked the roads of earth.

As a student of God here on earth, this man studied God's Word and hid it in his heart. He applied its precepts in dealing with his family and with those who have worked with him. Many are the times that he spent the night hours praying for the right solution to a particularly troubling "shauri." Yet it could not be said of him that "he was so heavenly-minded that he was no earthly good." (I would tell you where this quote originated if I knew. It was probably one of my Mom's since it sounds like her. She also used to tell me "What you are going to be, you are now becoming." And I keep thinking that I should ask her if it has happened yet.) When I read my Bible about men who walked with God, the image of my Dad comes to mind. He walked and talked with God on a daily basis. He didn't tell us that he did this, he simply did it and we could tell.

As a human being, my Dad is even-tempered, well-mannered, considerate, loving, and has a wonderful sense of humor. He winks, makes V-faces, and had the best looking smile. I like his nose. He loves to read a good novel by Zane Grey or Louis L'Amour and I have seen him read far into the night to see how it turned out. How good it was to know that he could enjoy forgetting his troubles and bury himself in a good "read"! Even more heart-warming were the times when he filled the house with the gorgeous aroma of hamburgers and cocoa in the early hours of the morning and all of us would follow our noses to the kitchen to have a post-midnight feast before going back to bed with full bellies. (Please don't tell the health nuts about this travesty of nutrition. They couldn't possibly know how many times I've remembered those moments of enjoying my family).

When I remember the human qualities of my Dad, I also think of strength and creativity. I really believe that my Dad can do anything, and build anything. If that isn't true, it doesn't matter; he certainly never caused me to waver in this belief.

Lord, it would be arrogant of me to think that you need a recommendation of this man, but I need to see the words on paper. I believe my Dad will brighten your day too when he steps onto your heavenly campus to spend eternity there with you. Please save a place there for those of us who have had the pleasure of loving him here on earth. We'd like to see him again when we too arrive to see you face to face. Thank you for this example of man walking with God here on earth. It gives us courage to carry on.

The following was written by Ruth Ann's husband, Herbert's son-in-law.

AFRICAN EULOGY
by Joe Miano

*African drum
African beat
Clears the mind
And tempts the feet.
On foreign shore
In a distant place,
A boy grew up
With an African tongue.
And in this land
Where the air is thin
He taught them
Of his God
And reared his kin.*

*Here, close to God
On the rift's rim
He built a school
Where children
Learned of Christ
Through example,
Love, and discipline*

*Marching closer
Always nearer–
African drum
Beating with fervour–*

Marching onward
To meet the Savior!
The life he led–
A prayer he taught:
"Make me Lord
To all—to all
I'll meet or
All I've met."

African Drum
Rhythm unending–
African drum
Faith unswerving!
With each smile
With each tear
Remembering Herbert
We are blest–
Teacher, friend, and mentor–
Steel and softness.

Africa Drum
African beat
March with him to God.
Clears the mind
Tempts the feet
March with him to God!

For Mildred the loss of Herbert was difficult. They had lived and shared life together for fifty-five years. They had shared the good times and bad times, the laughs and tears. Now she was alone. But, as was typical of Mildred, she soldiered on and for a time continued alone in their home in Sandwich. Later she moved to South Bend, Indiana, so she could be near Ruth Ann and Joc. They had purchased a home for Mildred that was just down the road a short distance. This gave her independence, but was close enough for them to keep an eye on her. Mildred volunteered at the school doing clerical work, which provided a good way for her to become acquainted with some of the local people and to continue feeling useful.

While in South Bend, Mildred developed heart disease that required open-heart surgery. She rallied quite well from this surgery.

Having seen the struggles of Herbert and Mildred in their retirement years, Ruth Ann and Joe realized they needed to take a harder look at their own plans. Up until this time they had worked for Christian schools that did not have retirement plans. They sent out resumes to public schools and accepted new positions in Oklahoma City.

Although Mildred was comfortably settled into her little home, it was felt she should be with them, so Ruth Ann and Joe bought a house with enough room for Mildred to move in. Shortly after the move, Mildred required further heart surgery—valve replacement this time. She did well after this surgery and continued living with the Mianos for another six years.

When Mildred was about eighty-eight, they noticed that she was experiencing short-term memory loss. Along with this problem she was having balancing difficulties and falling frequently. In one severe fall she broke her pelvis, a fall from which she never quite recovered. Eventually, Ruth Ann and Joe were advised that Mildred needed round-the-clock care in a nursing home. Her memory loss was diagnosed as being the result of several small strokes. Right across the street was an assisted living facility, but Mildred's condition was felt to be too severe for assisted living.

Ruth Ann and Joe had planned a trip to Sicily to visit his family. What to do? Mildred insisted they go, and since her physical condition appeared to be stable they left. Mildred died in the hospital while they were in Europe. Ruth Ann has had to deal with the guilt from making that decision, although in her heart of hearts she knows her mother understood and wanted her to go. Her biggest comfort is that her last words to her mother were, "Mom, you know I love you." And Mildred responded, "I know you do." Glenn and his wife, Tweet, rushed to Oklahoma City but did not arrive before Mildred died. They made arrangements for her body to be shipped to Somonauk, Illinois, and postponed the funeral until Ruth Ann and Joe returned.

Mildred had lived another twelve years after Herbert's death, but now they were reunited in a far better place. A brother and sister, her five children and twelve grandchildren, and fifteen great-grandchildren survived her. Mildred was buried next to Herbert in a beautiful country hillside cemetery very near their Somonauk United Presbyterian Church, and close to their good friends Ed and Ruth Ouland.

The following is from "A Christian Family, Lessons Learned… and the ideal way to learn them," by Gayle Downing Grass:

RAINBOWS

They made a rainbow of life for us all
Blending the colors so we could see
Each value and hue, red, yellow and blue
Had something to offer each destiny.

Several emotions bring red to attention:
Anger, embarrassment, punishment, pain,
Misunderstandings, rejections, corrections,
Oft' remembered, ourselves mostly to blame.

Yellow brings joy, warm sunshine and peace
This color mixed with others often will show
A little, a lot, or all of itself
Giving our lives a more comforting glow.

Blue are the moods life often brings
Discouragement, disappointments, departures,
Delays. Where should we turn?
Who is it controls mysterious futures?

Early examples taught us the way
Only on God should His children call,
He made the rainbow viewed high in the sky
So we would look up—see Him above all.

17.

Afterword

In 2001 I began making annual trips to Kenya, where I volunteered my services as a school psychologist at the Rift Valley Academy. The idea was to identify students who were struggling and through assessment suggest ways of helping teachers and parents know how to better assist the student.

Getting back to the old school and on familiar territory was exciting and nostalgic. Although the outside of the school was very familiar, and still stood looking over the beautiful Rift Valley far below, the interior was completely different. The exceptional growth in student body had required moving all student living quarters out of Kiambogo, the old building. What we used to call the front of the building was now considered the back. A whole new main entrance had been constructed on the back of the building leading to office space on the second floor that used to be the "boys' side." Actually the whole building had been gutted and all the fireplaces closed so that the chimneys were only reminders of days that used to be. The big swot room was now the *chai* room where faculty meets for daily prayer and announcements over a cup of morning tea. Pa Ken's office next door was a computer workshop where technicians monitored and fixed ailing equipment. The former library had become a workroom where teachers could get copies made. The kitchen and dining rooms were now housed in a whole new, and huge, building across a grassy quad from the new front of the old building. Upstairs where the homemakers' apartment and the girls' rooms had been was entirely office space, a nice conference room and even a restroom with flush toilets and running water. The floors were no longer wooden planks but polished hardwood.

What would Father Downing have thought of this development? When he knew RVA, this building was considered huge and expected to be more than adequate, forever. Now dormitories and classrooms scattered over several acres and a huge gymnasium and athletic fields attested to the explosive expansion of the school's academic and athletic excellence. A full elementary school stood up the hill where smaller children could begin their studies in an environment better suited to their needs. That school of six classrooms had been built under Herb Downing's regime, but even that had expanded with an office building attached at one end and an auditorium appropriately called Downing Hall at the other.

As I was shown to my workspace, which happened to be in the former boys' living room, I wondered how the Downings would have reacted. Perhaps they would experience it a little as I did, with mixed emotions and nostalgia. This generation of faculty and students had no idea what this old building used to look like inside nor the wonderful tales it could tell if only it could talk! They had not roller skated on the "front" porch or sneaked the opportunity to hold the hand of a boy or girlfriend while enjoying the view of the valley below. This new generation smirked each time I called that side facing the valley "front," when they knew it as back. How could they understand the feelings I experienced as I wandered through each room recalling the days that used to be? And then I thought, If I feel this way, how would it be for Lee and Blanche, Herb and Mildred, Ken and Ivy?

In 2006 I had the opportunity to take about 140 former students and their spouses from the United States back to the centennial reunion at RVA. There we met hundreds of others from around the world who came to celebrate the grand occasion. Now I found that my feelings and experiences were not unusual. Looking around the old place, we began to look for the familiar "old" landmarks. The much-photographed cornerstone laid by President Theodore Roosevelt was still there; the plaque over the door of the "big swot room" placed for Mrs. Butterworth, who had donated the money for the original building, was still in place. The old building from the exterior was much the same except the familiar wooden steps on the "front" of the building were long gone. The alumni decided to remedy that by donating money to replace the steps. John Barnett, a former student, who served on the faculty, undertook the project and rebuilt the steps at their original site with the same yellow limestone used for much of the construction of Kiambogo. John became ill and died in 2008, but he did live to see the steps completed. Those steps stand as a memorial to John Barnett and to the thousands of students who have traversed the halls of Rift Valley Academy and are now scattered all over the world using the education they received on the slopes of the Great Rift Valley.

I think the Lee, Herbert, and Kenneth Downings would be pleased and proud.

John Barnett and Mary Honer on the steps donated by alumni, with students Onna Harrison and Andrew Choi

Appendix 1: The Children

FOOTPRINTS

Lives of great men all remind us
We can make our lives sublime,
And, departing, leave behind us
Footprints on the sands of time;

From: *A Psalm of Life*
by Henry Wadsworth Longfellow (1807–1882)

The Children of
Herbert C. Downing and Mildred S. Houk Downing

Gayle Margaret Downing Grass was born in Allegheny County, Pennsylvania, on May 15, 1932. She graduated from RVA in 1950, went on to Barrington Bible College, in Barrington, Rhode Island, and then the University of Maine at Presque Isle, Maine, where she received her teaching credential. She taught school until she retired.

Kendall and Gayle Grass

Gayle married Kendall Gerard Grass on September 1, 1955. Kendall was born in Mars Hill, Aroostook County, Maine. He attended Barrington Bible College and the University of Maine, Presque Isle, Maine, receiving a BA. He was a teacher and farmer. They have a daughter, Fonda Jean, and three sons: Warren, Darren, and Sheldon.

Glenn Herbert Downing was born at Kijabe, Kenya, on January 22, 1935. He graduated from the Rift Valley Academy in 1952 and went on to continue his education at Barrington Bible College with a major in Christian education. He then joined the Marines and became a pilot. He was a professional pilot until his retirement.

On August 31, 1963, he married Thelma "Tweet" Marie Teuscher, a teacher. Tweet was born September 10, 1938. She attended Barrington College (formerly Providence Bible College), where she received her bachelor's degree and teaching certificate. Tweet's sister was Gayle Downing's roommate. For one year while Glenn was overseas Tweet taught fourth grade at RVA. Glenn and Tweet have three children: Ann Marie, Virginia, and Jonathan.

Glenn and Thelma "Tweet" Downing

Edwin Lee Downing was born in New Concord, Ohio, on October 24, 1937. He graduated from RVA in 1955, and for one year, 1955–56, he worked at the Kijabe store that served the local missionary families

Edwin and Lois Downing

and also the students. He went on to graduate from Wheaton College, Wheaton, Illinois, in 1960 with a BS and from the Jefferson Medical College, Philadelphia, Pennsyvania, with his MD in 1964. He then did his internship in the US Army Medical Corps at Tripler Medical Center, Honolulu, Hawaii, until 1965; was battalion surgeon in Hawaii and Vietnam 1965–66; and chief of clinics at Aberdeen Proving Ground, Maryland, 1967–68. He did his ophthalmology residency at Hines Loyola VA Hospital, Maywood, Illinois, 1968–71. He then went into private practice from 1971 to 2006. In retirement he is working as an assistant clinical professor of ophthalmology for the Wisconsin Eye Institute Medical College.

On June 8, 1963, he married Lois Rachel Epp, whose parents, Eldo and Verna, were missionaries in the Belgian Congo under Africa Inland Mission between 1937 and 1975. Lois was born May 12, 1940, at Rethy, Belgian Congo. She attended Rethy Academy, sister school to RVA, through tenth grade, and graduated from Wheaton Academy,

Wheaton, Illinois, in 1958. She received her RN in 1961 from West Suburban Hospital School of Nursing, Oak Park, Illinois, and in 1963 earned her BSN at University of Wisconsin Oshkosh College of Nursing, and her MSN from the same institution in 1987. She worked as a nurse practitioner and office manager in Ed's practice. They have two daughters: Brenda Lee and Sandra Ruth.

Ruth Ann Downing Miano was born in Zanesville, Ohio, April 18, 1942. She graduated from RVA in 1960 and went on to study at Wheaton, where she earned a BA in mathematics, minored in Latin and education, and received her teaching certification. She took nine hours of graduate study with the National Science Foundation at Notre Dame, South Bend, Indiana, and received a master's degree from Indiana University, also in

Joseph and Ruth Ann Miano

South Bend, in mathematics education. Ruth taught at William Hatch School in Oak Park, Illinois, for two years; Rift Valley Academy for two years; and Mitchell School in Racine, Wisconsin, for one year. She also taught at the International School of Kenya in Nairobi for eight years and St. Joseph High School in South Bend, Indiana, for twelve years. Currently she has completed nineteen years teaching at Casady School in Oklahoma City, Oklahoma. She is the head of the math department and has taught everything from Algebra I to BC Calculus.

Ruth Ann married Joseph S. Miano in 1976 in Nairobi, Kenya. Joe attended Dumont High School, Dumont, New Jersey. He then went to Fairleigh Dickinson, Teaneck, New Jersey, 1966–67, and the University of Rochester, Rochester, New York, where he received his BS in physics. Then he went to the University of Notre Dame, where he received a MS in nuclear physics in 1972. Over the next decade and more, he taught chemistry, physics, and/or math. He joined the Peace Corps and worked in Nkubu High School, in Meru, Kenya, 1972–75. He went on to the International School of Kenya in Nairobi, Kenya, where he was chair of the science department. Between 1976 and 1977, he taught at the United States International University, Nairobi. Between 1979 and 1982, he taught at Marian

High School in Mishawaka, Indiana. He returned to the University of Notre Dame, St. Mary's College, Indiana, receiving his teaching certificate in 1982. He received a life certificate in 1986, with a physics major and a math and chemistry minor. Then he taught at St. Joseph's High School 1982 to 1990, in South Bend, Indiana, where he was chair of the science department. From 1990 to the present, he and Ruth Ann have been teaching at Casady School, Oklahoma City, Oklahoma, where he is chair of the science department.

John Martin Downing was born in Ohio on March 20, 1953. Before his first birthday his family took him to Kenya. Martin graduated from RVA in July 1971. He attended Geneva College in Beaver Falls, Pennsylvania, where he majored in biology and received his BS. After college he worked for thirteen years as a

Martin and Norma Downing

cardiovascular technician in Fairfax, Virginia. He then went back to school at Johns Hopkins University, Baltimore, Maryland, where he received his certificate as a cardiovascular perfusionist. He has been working in that capacity in Concord, North Carolina, until the present.

Martin married Norma Jane Troup on August 18, 1979. Norma was born in Hackensack, New Jersey, February 13, 1958. She also attended Geneva College and the University of North Carolina, Chapel Hill, North Carolina, and earned her BS in chemistry. They have three children: John Mark, Susanna, and Joseph. After the children were grown, she returned to school and received her BN.

The Children of
Kenneth Lee Downing and Ivy Ambrose Downing

Daphne Blanche Downing McRostie was born April 8, 1938, in Nairobi, Kenya. She graduated from RVA in 1955. She attended Barrington College in Barrington, Rhode Island, between 1956 and 1958, with a major in Bible and Nursing. She then went on to West Suburban Hospital of Nursing in Oak Park, Illinois, where she received her RN. Between 1961 and 1964 Daphne worked as an office nurse for Dr. Everett Nicholas, who was a general surgeon in Oak Park, Illinois. She then joined the

Gordon and Daphne McRostie

Gospel Missionary Union (now called Avant Ministries) and went to Morocco, Belgium, and Spain. She and Gordon served together in Morocco for many years.

On July 10, 1965, she married Gordon McRostie, in Neuchatel, Switzerland. They had four children: Cyndi Ann, Kenneth, Marcie Lee, and Stephen. Marcie died when six years of age.

David William Downing was born August 11, 1940, at Oicha, in the Belgian Congo. The attending physician was the famous Dr. Becker of Africa Inland Mission. David graduated from RVA in 1958 and went on to study at the Moody Bible Institute, Chicago, Illinois, where he took a pastor's course. He then went to Northern Illinois University, DeKalb, Illinois, where he studied chemistry. With the AIM he served in Zaire 1969–1991, with World Concern 1993–2002, and GYF (Go Ye Fellowship) 2002–2008.

David Downing

In August 1964, he married Diane Ruth Casselman, RN, and together they served in the Congo as missionaries. That marriage ended in divorce in 1993.

They had three children: Dawn Lisa, Diane Michelle, and David Scott. He then married Faith Kanini Masila in April of 1996. They had two children: Matthew Masila and Lillian Kakeni Deborah. Faith died in December 2000 and is buried at the little cemetery at Kijabe where David's parents and grandparents are also interred. In 2002 he married Brendah Tembulah Masinde, but that marriage ended in divorce in 2007. They had no children. David calls himself a semi-retired missionary who is currently working at Wal-Mart in Siloam Springs, Arkansas.

Dorothy Ann Downing Hildebrandt was born on November 8,

1943, at the Maia Carberry Nursing Home in Nairobi, Kenya. She graduated from RVA in 1961 and went to the Freeman Business College, Oak Park, Illinois, then on to Columbia Bible College in Columbia, South Carolina, where she majored in Biblical education.

Dottie and Jonathan Arnold Hildebrandt were married in the Ziwani Africa Inland Church in Nairobi on December 29, 1973. Jonathan was born May 2, 1942,

Jonathan and Dorothy Hildebrandt

in Montclair, New Jersey. He is the grandson of missionaries who served in West Africa and in the United States. His father was a math professor at Northwestern University, Evanston, Illinois, and his mother was an English teacher. He also attended RVA; New Trier High School in Winnetka, Illinois, where he graduated; Taylor University, Upland, Indiana, 1960–62; Northwestern University, 1962–64 and 1966–67; Columbia University, New York, 1964; and Trinity Evangelical Divinity School, Deerfield, Illinois, 1967–68. He has a BS in education and an MA in African history. Jonathan taught at Mang'u High School, Thika, Kenya, under the Teachers for East Africa Program, 1964–66. Dottie and Jonathan were accepted by AIM and went to Kenya in December 1968. They have served thirty-six years in Kenya and four in Australia. Jonathan has been a teacher and administrator for forty years with AIM. They have two sons: Jon Philip and Paul Kenneth. Dottie and Jonathan retired to the Africa Inland Mission Retirement Center, Media, in Minneola, Florida.

Lee Herbert Downing was born at the Maia Carberry Nursing Home in Nairobi, Kenya on December 26, 1948. He graduated from RVA July 1967. He attended Columbia Bible College, Columbia, South Carolina, between 1967 and 1969. He then went to Pan American University between 1980 and 1981, after which he continued his studies at Pittsburgh Institute of Aeronautics, West Mifflin, Pennsylvania, between 1981 and 1983. Lee was employed by the United States Air Force between 1970 and 1973. He joined the Air National Guard, where he

Lee and Lu Downing

served 1981–2004. Between 1974 and 1981, he was a cross-country truck driver and dispatcher. Since 1983 he has worked as a mechanic for Continental Airlines.

Lee married Lula Mae Fuchs, known as Lu, on January 31, 1976. Lu has taught piano and been an accompanist and a missionary to Haiti. They have two sons, David and Dean, and a daughter, Debbie, who was killed in an auto accident when she was eighteen. Lee and Lu live in Colorado, where they intend to spend the rest of their lives.

Victor Kenneth Downing was born May 10, 1950, at the Maia Carberry Nursing Home in Nairobi, Kenya. He graduated from RVA in 1968 and attended Taylor University, Upland, Indiana, where he earned a BA in Biblical literature in 1974. He then went to Trinity Evangelical Divinity School, Deerfield, Illinois, where he earned an MA in Biblical Studies. He went on to Drew University, Madison, New Jersey, where he got a Ph.D. in theological and

Vic Downing

Biblical studies. Vic served as a pastor for twenty-four years and then as a health care chaplain from 2006 to the present.

He was married to Lynda Myers from 1974 to 2004 and is currently married to Jeanne Jeska, whom he married in 2006. He has four children: Daniel, James, Stephanie, and Joseph.

Appendix 2: How May I Know God's Plan For My Life?
by Rev. Lee H. Downing

Do you know that He has a plan—a plan for your life as definite as that of the architect for a building about to be erected? Before a stone of the foundation is laid the architect has thought through the prepared detail specifications regarding the shape and size of the building and of every piece of material entering into its construction. God's plan for your life is not less definite, and His plan is the best that could possibly be made. He understands you better than you understand yourself, knows your limitations and your capabilities better than you know them, and knows also conditions throughout the world, not only those that prevail at the present moment, but all that will arise until the end of time. Is He not, therefore best qualified to order your life? This He waits to do.

Somewhere in this world He has prepared a niche for you, and when you find the niche you will fit into it as you will into no other. Richer experiences await you there than elsewhere in all the world. "Strength and gladness are in his place" (I Chron. 16:27) "His place" for you, therefore is the one in which you will be strongest and happiest, the one in which you will experience the highest degree of joy and satisfaction and fruitfulness in service of which you are capable.

Dr. F.B. Meyer once expressed the thought that if such a thing as sorrow were possible in heaven, a sufficient cause for it would be to have God's draft-plan for an individual produced before him that he might compare what God had intended him to do with what he had actually accomplished. The contrast, Dr. Meyer believed, would be so striking as to cause sorrow, if that were possible up there.

How May I Know God's Plan For My Life?

To some the answer has come through pursuing the course prescribed in the following outline, supported by the Scripture texts inserted:

1. Be assured that He has a plan.
   Eph. 2:10; Acts 15:18; Ps. 37:23; Phil. 2:13; Acts 13:2.

2. Be assured that He will reveal His plan.
    Eph. 5:17; Col. 1:9; Ps. 32:8; Ps. 73:24; Acts 16:6.7.
3. Afford Him an opportunity by waiting upon Him.
    (a) Alone. Matt. 6:6.
    (b) At an appointed time.
    (c) With your whole being yielded to Him. Rom.12:1, 2.
    (d) In expectancy—faith. Heb. 11:6.
    (e) Recording the impressions.
    (f) Begin to execute the plan as soon as it is revealed.
4. Acts 26:19.20.

1. Be Assured That He Has a Plan.

This is important, for the Adversary knows that God will be more glorified through our executing His plan for our lives than in the accomplishment of any self-chosen tasks. Therefore he will do his utmost to prevent our knowing the plan, and only a well-grounded assurance of its existence will enable us to persevere until the revelation comes. Such assurance may be had through accepting the truth stated in the texts and cited above, only one of which will be commented upon.

Ephesians 2:10 declares that "We are … created in Christ Jesus unto good works, which God hath before ordained (R.V., 'prepared') that we could walk in them." How long "before," is suggested by the clause in Eph. 1:4, "Chosen" … in him before the foundation of the world. Wondrous thought, that we should be in God's mind, and our lives be planned, before this universe was brought into being! But we are of more value to Him than the material world about us, and it is because we cost Him more.

"That we should walk in them" is the final statement of the verse quoted above—language which suggests that before each of us is a divinely prepared pathway strewn with good works made ready to our hands. Along the one prepared for you will be found all the souls He expects you to win, all the work He expects you to accomplish, and all the discipline necessary to fit you for that work. What if you miss that pathway? You will miss God's best for you, and enjoy only His second choice.

"God has His best things for the few
   That dare to stand the test;
God has His second choice for those
   Who will not have His best."

Having become assured that He has a plan for your life, next be assured

2. That He Will Reveal to You That Plan.

"Be not unwise, but understanding what the will of the Lord is." We are commanded to know His will, therefore it must be His will to reveal His will, including the part which concerns your life work.

"That ye might be filled with the knowledge of his will" is one petition in the apostle's prayer for the saints of Colosse. When we are filled with the knowledge of His will, there is no place left for doubt and uncertainty.

Turning to the American Revised Version one finds this interesting series of texts: "Counsel is mine" (Prov. 8:14), "I will counsel thee" (Ps. 32:8), "The counsel of Jehovah standeth fast for ever" (Ps. 33:11). The marginal rendering in this version of Prov. 8:14 affords a powerful incentive to have one's life ordered by the Lord. It is this: "Counsel is mine, and effectual working: I am understanding; I have might." Get your counsel from God, and He is the Effectual Worker to bring it to pass. He is able to place you where He wants you. The principalities and powers opposed the risen Savior's return to the Father's right hand, but He brought Him triumphantly through these organized forces of evil arrayed against Him and placed Him just where He wanted Him. He will do as much for you—that is, He will place you just where He wants you—when your life is wholly at His disposal.

Do not these Scriptures assure you that God has a plan for your life, and that He has pledged Himself to reveal that plan if you will fulfill his conditions? If so, then

3. Afford Him an Opportunity by Waiting Upon Him.

(a) *Alone*. Jesus said, "Thou, when thou prayest, enter into thy closet, and when thou has shut thy door, pray to they Father which is in secret; and thy Father which seeth in secret shall reward thee openly." In the secret place, shut in with God, we may expect leadings so definite as to assure others later that they were from Him.

When I announced my decision to go to Africa, some friends sought to dissuade me. They knew I was not very strong physically, though passed by the doctor, and to them it seemed a great risk, especially to go under a Faith Mission, which does not guarantee the support of its missionaries. Now, after twenty-three years of service on the field, with every need supplied, not one of them feels that I made a mistake. Little did I realize, as I waited for guidance day after day in the secret place, that the Father would ever reward me so "openly."

"He shall bring forth ... thy judgment as the noonday" (Ps. 37:6) was verified in my experience.

(b) *At an appointed time.* Think over your daily schedule and decide when in the twenty-four hours you could be alone with the Lord without interruption, and make up your mind to **meet Him every day at that time**. The duration of the interview will be determined somewhat by the other duties demanding your attention. A half-hour *daily*, if more cannot be spared, is better than an hour today, no time tomorrow, and such time the day following as can be conveniently spent in this way. The faithful keeping of this appointment prepares one to receive impressions from the Lord, and brings the consciousness of having definite dealing with Him.

(c) *With your whole being yield to Him.* This is an absolute necessity. The one who, on hearing that God has a plan for every life, says, "I would like to look over His plan for me to see if I will accept it," will finish his days down here without having seen the plan. God never promised to reveal it on such terms. It is after the body has been presented a living sacrifice that God's will becomes "acceptable" (Rom. 12:1,2).

The experience of a young man in the University of Minnesota illustrates this truth. He was wanted on the varsity football team and wanted as a manager of a branch store by the firm for which he had been working, but God was claiming his life. One evening as the sun was setting, four of us who had spent the day together in his home city went to a nearby place on the shore on Lake Superior and seated ourselves for prayer on a large rock which jutted out a little way into the water. The other three had prayed and he began, but his throat filled; the tears started and the voice stopped; be began to sob and his big body shook with emotion. After a brief silence he said, "Fellows, forgive me, I cannot help it " Isaiah 57:15 was quoted to assure him that his present condition was pleasing to God. "For thus saith the high and lofty One that inhabiteth eternity, whose name is Holy; I dwell in the high and holy place, with him also that is of a contrite and humble spirit, to revive the spirit of the humble, and to revive the heart of the contrite one." He resumed praying and said, "Lord Thou didst never have me before this evening. Take me and use me in any way that will serve Thy purpose." From that moment he desired above everything else to know God's will. Nothing was now so "acceptable" to him, but this experience followed that of presenting his body a living sacrifice.

(d) *In expectancy—faith.* "Without faith it is impossible to please him: for he that cometh to God must believe that he is, and that he is a rewarder of them that diligently seek him." In order therefore to know His plan, one must come to Him in faith, but the faith which He requires He is ready to impart through the means mentioned in Rom. 10:17: "Faith cometh by hearing, and hearing by the word of God." As well might one hope to maintain physical strength without partaking of wholesome food, as to possess faith without pondering the Word of God. The doctor's method of restoring health to an invalid illustrates God's usual method of imparting faith to His children. Specific directions are given by the doctor regarding diet, drugs, exercise, rest, and everything that affects the patient's condition. Through the faithful observance of his directions health is restored. The process may involve months of living strictly in accord with the doctor's orders—abstaining from foods that are prohibited, though pleasing to the palate; retiring at the appropriate hour, though further fellowship with friends would be very enjoyable; taking bitter tonics because they are prescribed; and doing other things which the flesh would rather not do—but no self-denial is deemed too great if only health can be restored.

So with faith. It is imparted gradually through ordering the life strictly in accord with the teaching of God's Word. Most people are unwilling to pay the price of faith. They want to receive it in bulk form, as it were, and without cost or delay.

(e) *Recording the impressions.* Just how God's plan for a particular life will be revealed, no one can say. He does not deal alike with His children, but each may be lead on to prayer experiences too rich to be described, and too sacred to be divulged. "If I tried, I could not utter what He says when thus we meet" is the language of every soul accustomed to frequent and sometimes prolonged sessions alone with Him.

My only hope, therefore is to say something of a general character that may help those who are just beginning to seek counsel of God.

The simple suggestion, made many years ago to a group of Bible students by the General Director of our Mission (the man who by precept and example has helped me more than any other toward a life of absolute dependence upon God), I hope will prove as helpful to you as it has been to me.

When desirous of knowing God's will concerning an important matter, especially if it be whether or not you should do a particular thing, draw a line through a blank sheet of paper, and on one side of the line write all the reasons for and on the other side all the reasons against doing the thing. Pray over these reasons. If necessary revise the list from day to day while alone with Him at the appointed time. Ere long quite a distinct impression will be borne in upon your heart in favor of one side or the other. If the impression which comes today is from the Spirit of God, it will be deeper tomorrow; if not from Him, it will fade out. We should, I believe, regard as from the Lord the impressions that come to us when we are alone with Him and absolutely yielded, i.e., perfectly willing to do or not to do the thing about which we are inquiring. An earthly father would not consent to an enemy's answering the question of his son who comes to him for advice; nor will our heavenly Father permit His enemy to enter the secret place and influence the child who is so eager to know His will as to set apart a time and go alone daily to receive the revelation of it. One needs, I know, to speak guardedly of it. It is easy to become presumptuous and fanatical, but let us remember that we are in God's school, pupils to be taught individually by His Spirit and then seek to discover His method of influencing us personally. I am not emotional; I do not have visions, or hear audible voices, or have such spectacular experiences as I have heard others relate. In my experience the leading comes through gradually deepening inward impressions such as I have already described. Time will reveal to us and others whether or not we have learned to discern His presence, and to understand His impressions.

Here our study ends. Has it been worthwhile? Are you yet sure that God has a plan for your life, and that you may know it? Has any revelation come as to the way? If so, praise Him, and tell Him you are willing to pay the price of knowing the plan, if only you may have the satisfaction of being consciously in His appointed place, and doing the specific work for which He brought you into the world.

Published 1952 by Africa Inland Mission; on the flyleaf:

"Rev. Lee H. Downing
was a missionary of the
Africa Inland Mission
laboring in Kenya from 1901
till his death in 1942."

Appendix 3: Downing Genealogy

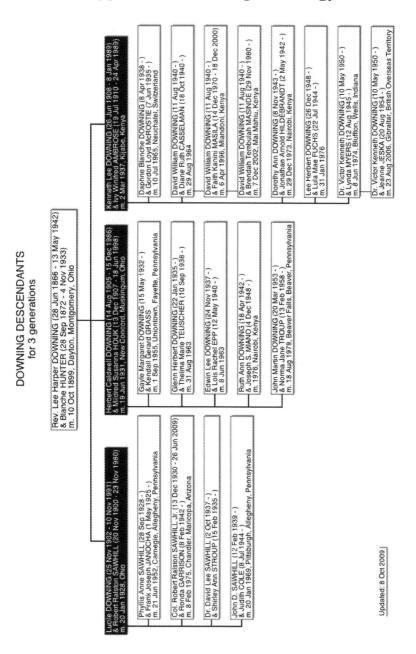

DOWNING DESCENDANTS for 3 generations

Rev. Lee Harper DOWNING (28 Jun 1866 - 13 May 1942)
& Blanche HUNTER (28 Sep 1872 - 4 Nov 1933)
m. 10 Oct 1899, Dayton, Montgomery, Ohio

Lucie DOWNING (25 Nov 1902 - 10 Nov 1991)
& Robert Ralston SAWHILL (20 Nov 1900 - 23 Nov 1980)
m. 20 Jan 1928, Ohio

Phyllis Anne SAWHILL (28 Sep 1928 -)
& Frank Joseph JANOCHA (1 May 1925 -)
m. 21 Jun 1952, Carnegie, Allegheny, Pennsylvania

Col. Robert Ralston SAWHILL Jr. (13 Dec 1930 - 26 Jun 2009)
& Ronda GARRISON (8 Feb 1942 -)
m. 8 Feb 1975, Chandler, Maricopa, Arizona

Dr. David Lee SAWHILL (2 Oct 1937 -)
& Shirley Ann STROUP (15 Feb 1935 -)

John D. SAWHILL (12 Feb 1939 -)
& Judith COLE (8 Jul 1944 -)
m. 20 Jan 1969, Pittsburgh, Allegheny, Pennsylvania

Herbert Caldwell DOWNING (14 Aug 1905 - 15 Dec 1986)
& Mildred Susanna HOUK (13 Dec 1907 - 18 Jun 1998)
m. 19 Jun 1931, New Concord, Muskingum, Ohio

Gayle Margaret DOWNING (15 May 1932 -)
& Kendall Gerard GRASS
m. 1 Sep 1955, Uniontown, Fayette, Pennsylvania

Glenn Herbert DOWNING (22 Jan 1935 -)
& Thelma Marie TEUSCHER (10 Sep 1938 -)
m. 31 Aug 1963

Edwin Lee DOWNING (24 Nov 1937 -)
& Lois Rachel EPP (12 May 1940 -)
m. 8 Jun 1963

Ruth Ann DOWNING (18 Apr 1942 -)
& Joseph S. MIANO (4 Dec 1948 -)
m. 1976, Nairobi, Kenya

John Martin DOWNING (20 Mar 1953 -)
& Norma Jane TROUP (13 Feb 1958 -)
m. 18 Aug 1979, Beaver Falls, Beaver, Pennsylvania

Kenneth Lee DOWNING (26 Jun 1908 - 8 Jan 1989)
& Ivy Winifred AMBROSE (19 Jul 1910 - 24 Apr 1989)
m. 2 Mar 1937, Kijabe, Kenya

Daphne Blanche DOWNING (8 Apr 1938 -)
& Gordon Loyd McFROSTIE (7 Jun 1935 -)
m. 10 Jul 1965, Neuchatel, Switzerland

David William DOWNING (11 Aug 1940 -)
& Diane Ruth CASSELMAN (18 Oct 1940 -)
m. 29 Aug 1984

David William DOWNING (11 Aug 1940 -)
& Faith Kanini MASILA (14 Dec 1970 - 18 Dec 2000)
m. 6 Apr 1996, Miandoni, Kenya

David William DOWNING (11 Aug 1940 -)
& Brendah Tembulah MASINDE (29 Nov 1980 -)
m. 7 Dec 2002, Mai Mahiu, Kenya

Dorothy Ann DOWNING (8 Nov 1943 -)
& Jonathan Arnold HILDEBRANDT (2 May 1942 -)
m. 29 Dec 1973, Nairobi, Kenya

Lee Herbert DOWNING (26 Dec 1948 -)
& Lula Mae FUCHS (22 Jul 1944 -)
m. 31 Jan 1976

Dr. Victor Kenneth DOWNING (10 May 1950 -)
& Lynda MYERS (12 Aug 1945 -)
m. 8 Jun 1974, Bluffton, Wells, Indiana

Dr. Victor Kenneth DOWNING (10 May 1950 -)
& Jeanne JESKA (20 Aug 1954 -)
m. 23 Aug 2006, Gibraltar, British Overseas Territory

Updated: 8 Oct 2009

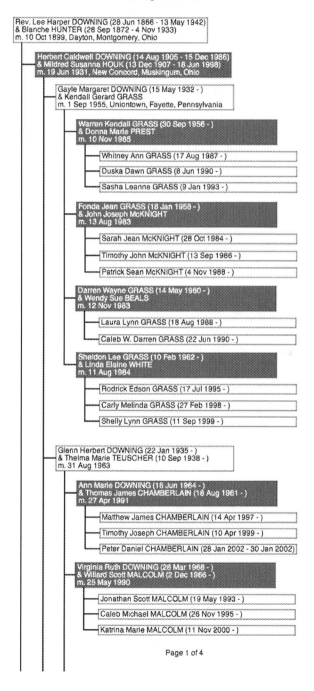

Rev. Lee Harper DOWNING (28 Jun 1866 - 13 May 1942)
& Blanche HUNTER (28 Sep 1872 - 4 Nov 1933)
m. 10 Oct 1899, Dayton, Montgomery, Ohio

Herbert Caldwell DOWNING (14 Aug 1905 - 15 Dec 1986)
& Mildred Susanna HOUK (13 Dec 1907 - 18 Jun 1998)
m. 19 Jun 1931, New Concord, Muskingum, Ohio

Gayle Margaret DOWNING (15 May 1932 -)
& Kendall Gerard GRASS
m. 1 Sep 1955, Uniontown, Fayette, Pennsylvania

Warren Kendall GRASS (30 Sep 1956 -)
& Donna Marie PREST
m. 10 Nov 1985

Whitney Ann GRASS (17 Aug 1987 -)

Duska Dawn GRASS (8 Jun 1990 -)

Sasha Leanne GRASS (9 Jan 1993 -)

Fonda Jean GRASS (18 Jan 1958 -)
& John Joseph McKNIGHT
m. 13 Aug 1983

Sarah Jean McKNIGHT (28 Oct 1984 -)

Timothy John McKNIGHT (13 Sep 1986 -)

Patrick Sean McKNIGHT (4 Nov 1988 -)

Darren Wayne GRASS (14 May 1960 -)
& Wendy Sue BEALS
m. 12 Nov 1983

Laura Lynn GRASS (18 Aug 1988 -)

Caleb W. Darren GRASS (22 Jun 1990 -)

Sheldon Lee GRASS (10 Feb 1962 -)
& Linda Elaine WHITE
m. 11 Aug 1984

Rodrick Edson GRASS (17 Jul 1995 -)

Carly Melinda GRASS (27 Feb 1998 -)

Shelly Lynn GRASS (11 Sep 1999 -)

Glenn Herbert DOWNING (22 Jan 1935 -)
& Thelma Marie TEUSCHER (10 Sep 1938 -)
m. 31 Aug 1963

Ann Marie DOWNING (16 Jun 1964 -)
& Thomas James CHAMBERLAIN (16 Aug 1961 -)
m. 27 Apr 1991

Matthew James CHAMBERLAIN (14 Apr 1997 -)

Timothy Joseph CHAMBERLAIN (10 Apr 1999 -)

Peter Daniel CHAMBERLAIN (28 Jan 2002 - 30 Jan 2002)

Virginia Ruth DOWNING (28 Mar 1968 -)
& Willard Scott MALCOLM (2 Dec 1966 -)
m. 25 May 1990

Jonathan Scott MALCOLM (19 May 1993 -)

Caleb Michael MALCOLM (26 Nov 1995 -)

Katrina Marie MALCOLM (11 Nov 2000 -)

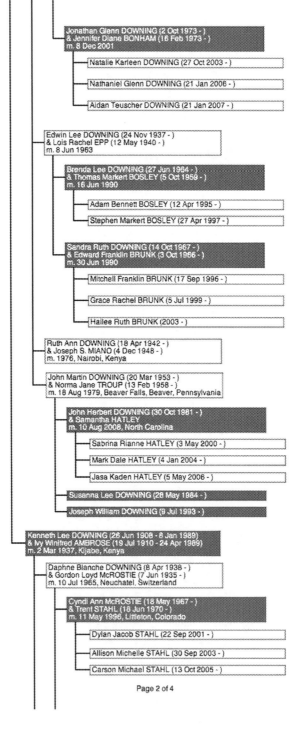

Jonathan Glenn DOWNING (2 Oct 1973 -)
& Jennifer Diane BONHAM (16 Feb 1973 -)
m. 8 Dec 2001

Natalie Karleen DOWNING (27 Oct 2003 -)

Nathaniel Glenn DOWNING (21 Jan 2006 -)

Aidan Teuscher DOWNING (21 Jan 2007 -)

Edwin Lee DOWNING (24 Nov 1937 -)
& Lois Rachel EPP (12 May 1940 -)
m. 8 Jun 1963

Brenda Lee DOWNING (27 Jun 1964 -)
& Thomas Markert BOSLEY (5 Oct 1959 -)
m. 16 Jun 1990

Adam Bennett BOSLEY (12 Apr 1995 -)

Stephen Markert BOSLEY (27 Apr 1997 -)

Sandra Ruth DOWNING (14 Oct 1967 -)
& Edward Franklin BRUNK (3 Oct 1966 -)
m. 30 Jun 1990

Mitchell Franklin BRUNK (17 Sep 1996 -)

Grace Rachel BRUNK (5 Jul 1999 -)

Hailee Ruth BRUNK (2003 -)

Ruth Ann DOWNING (18 Apr 1942 -)
& Joseph S. MIANO (4 Dec 1948 -)
m. 1976, Nairobi, Kenya

John Martin DOWNING (20 Mar 1953 -)
& Norma Jane TROUP (13 Feb 1958 -)
m. 18 Aug 1979, Beaver Falls, Beaver, Pennsylvania

John Herbert DOWNING (30 Oct 1981 -)
& Samantha HATLEY
m. 10 Aug 2008, North Carolina

Sabrina Rianne HATLEY (3 May 2000 -)

Mark Dale HATLEY (4 Jan 2004 -)

Jasa Kaden HATLEY (5 May 2006 -)

Susanna Lee DOWNING (28 May 1984 -)

Joseph William DOWNING (9 Jul 1993 -)

Kenneth Lee DOWNING (26 Jun 1908 - 8 Jan 1989)
& Ivy Winifred AMBROSE (19 Jul 1910 - 24 Apr 1989)
m. 2 Mar 1937, Kijabe, Kenya

Daphne Blanche DOWNING (8 Apr 1938 -)
& Gordon Loyd McROSTIE (7 Jun 1935 -)
m. 10 Jul 1965, Neuchatel, Switzerland

Cyndi Ann McROSTIE (18 May 1967 -)
& Trent STAHL (18 Jun 1970 -)
m. 11 May 1996, Littleton, Colorado

Dylan Jacob STAHL (22 Sep 2001 -)

Allison Michelle STAHL (30 Sep 2003 -)

Carson Michael STAHL (13 Oct 2005 -)

Page 2 of 4

160

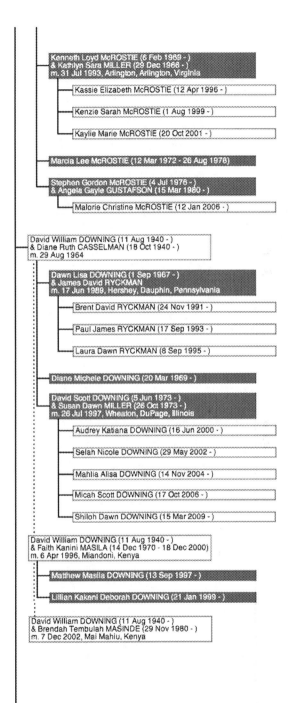

Kenneth Loyd McROSTIE (6 Feb 1969 -)
& Kathlyn Sara MILLER (29 Dec 1966 -)
m. 31 Jul 1993, Arlington, Arlington, Virginia

Kassie Elizabeth McROSTIE (12 Apr 1996 -)

Kenzie Sarah McROSTIE (1 Aug 1999 -)

Kaylie Marie McROSTIE (20 Oct 2001 -)

Marcia Lee McROSTIE (12 Mar 1972 - 26 Aug 1976)

Stephen Gordon McROSTIE (4 Jul 1976 -)
& Angela Gayle GUSTAFSON (15 Mar 1980 -)

Malorie Christine McROSTIE (12 Jan 2006 -)

David William DOWNING (11 Aug 1940 -)
& Diane Ruth CASSELMAN (18 Oct 1940 -)
m. 29 Aug 1964

Dawn Lisa DOWNING (1 Sep 1967 -)
& James David RYCKMAN
m. 17 Jun 1989, Hershey, Dauphin, Pennsylvania

Brent David RYCKMAN (24 Nov 1991 -)

Paul James RYCKMAN (17 Sep 1993 -)

Laura Dawn RYCKMAN (8 Sep 1995 -)

Diane Michele DOWNING (20 Mar 1969 -)

David Scott DOWNING (5 Jun 1973 -)
& Susan Dawn MILLER (26 Oct 1973 -)
m. 26 Jul 1997, Wheaton, DuPage, Illinois

Audrey Katiana DOWNING (16 Jun 2000 -)

Selah Nicole DOWNING (29 May 2002 -)

Mahlia Alisa DOWNING (14 Nov 2004 -)

Micah Scott DOWNING (17 Oct 2006 -)

Shiloh Dawn DOWNING (15 Mar 2009 -)

David William DOWNING (11 Aug 1940 -)
& Faith Kanini MASILA (14 Dec 1970 - 18 Dec 2000)
m. 6 Apr 1996, Miandoni, Kenya

Matthew Masila DOWNING (13 Sep 1997 -)

Lillian Kakeni Deborah DOWNING (21 Jan 1999 -)

David William DOWNING (11 Aug 1940 -)
& Brendah Tembulah MASINDE (29 Nov 1980 -)
m. 7 Dec 2002, Mai Mahiu, Kenya

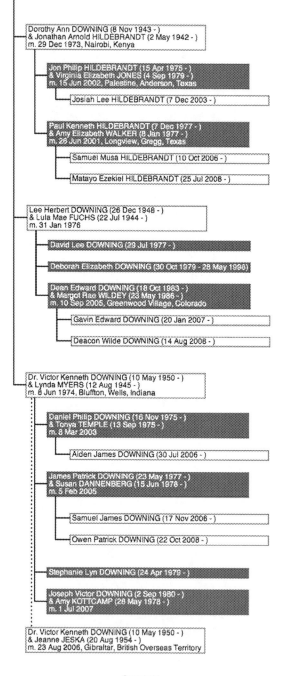

Dorothy Ann DOWNING (8 Nov 1943 -)
& Jonathan Arnold HILDEBRANDT (2 May 1942 -)
m. 29 Dec 1973, Nairobi, Kenya

Jon Philip HILDEBRANDT (15 Apr 1975 -)
& Virginia Elizabeth JONES (4 Sep 1979 -)
m. 15 Jun 2002, Palestine, Anderson, Texas

Josiah Lee HILDEBRANDT (7 Dec 2003 -)

Paul Kenneth HILDEBRANDT (7 Dec 1977 -)
& Amy Elizabeth WALKER (6 Jan 1977 -)
m. 26 Jun 2001, Longview, Gregg, Texas

Samuel Musa HILDEBRANDT (10 Oct 2006 -)

Matayo Ezekiel HILDEBRANDT (25 Jul 2008 -)

Lee Herbert DOWNING (26 Dec 1948 -)
& Lula Mae FUCHS (22 Jul 1944 -)
m. 31 Jan 1976

David Lee DOWNING (29 Jul 1977 -)

Deborah Elizabeth DOWNING (30 Oct 1979 - 28 May 1996)

Dean Edward DOWNING (18 Oct 1983 -)
& Margot Rae WILDEY (23 May 1986 -)
m. 10 Sep 2005, Greenwood Village, Colorado

Gavin Edward DOWNING (20 Jan 2007 -)

Deacon Wilde DOWNING (14 Aug 2008 -)

Dr. Victor Kenneth DOWNING (10 May 1950 -)
& Lynda MYERS (12 Aug 1945 -)
m. 8 Jun 1974, Bluffton, Wells, Indiana

Daniel Philip DOWNING (16 Nov 1975 -)
& Tonya TEMPLE (13 Sep 1975 -)
m. 8 Mar 2003

Aiden James DOWNING (30 Jul 2006 -)

James Patrick DOWNING (23 May 1977 -)
& Susan DANNENBERG (15 Jun 1978 -)
m. 5 Feb 2005

Samuel James DOWNING (17 Nov 2006 -)

Owen Patrick DOWNING (22 Oct 2008 -)

Stephanie Lyn DOWNING (24 Apr 1978 -)

Joseph Victor DOWNING (2 Sep 1980 -)
& Amy KOTTCAMP (28 May 1978 -)
m. 1 Jul 2007

Dr. Victor Kenneth DOWNING (10 May 1950 -)
& Jeanne JESKA (20 Aug 1954 -)
m. 23 Aug 2006, Gibraltar, British Overseas Territory

Glossary

Kiswahili words as used in the context of this book

americani a lightweight, unbleached muslin with many uses from ceilings to *shukas* to underwear in the early 1900s

baraza a meeting, reception, public audience, court of law, council, or meeting of elders of the tribe

chai tea, usually made by boiling milk and sugar together with water and tea leaves

duka shop or a stall

fundi craftsman, a person skilled in any art, craft, or profession, and so able to instruct others in it

maridufu a heavier weight of unbleached muslin

kipandi a card used for identification purposes

mabati corrugated iron, most often used for roofing

mbogo Cape buffalo

mzee old person, elder, used as a term of respect for a person of stature in the community

mzungu a European, commonly used for any white person

shauri problem

shuka a length of *americani* worn tied on one shoulder toga-style

About the Author

Mary Andersen Honer

Mary Honer was born in Kenya and grew up on Kijabe mission station, right among some of the families described in this story. She attended Rift Valley Academy (RVA) from first grade through part of ninth grade. After completing high school in California, she went to California State University, Long Beach, where she met her husband, Ted. After graduation, they went to Kenya and taught at RVA for seven years.

When they returned to California, Mary earned two master's degrees in education from California State University Fullerton, with specialties in reading and counseling, and went on to earn her doctorate at Brigham Young University in educational psychology.

Her career in California public schools covered teaching, counseling, and school psychology.

Since retiring, her calling to missionaries' children takes her to international and mission schools around the world, including RVA, where she uses her skills as a school psychologist, helping identify learning disabilities and better ways of meeting educational needs of this population of students.

Index of Names